Reviews and Essays, 1936–55

Poets on Poetry   *Donald Hall, General Editor*

Weldon Kees

Reviews and Essays, 1936–55

Edited by James Reidel
Introduction by Howard Nemerov

Ann Arbor
The University of Michigan Press

1991   1990   1989   1988   4   3   2   1

*Every effort has been made to trace the ownership of all
copyrighted material in this book and to obtain permission for its use.*

Library of Congress Cataloging-in-Publication Data

Kees, Weldon, 1914–1955?
    [Selections.   1988]
    Reviews and essays, 1936-55 / Weldon Kees ; edited by James Reidel ;
introduction by Howard Nemerov.
        p.   cm. — (Poets on poetry)
    ISBN 0-472-09383-5 (alk. paper)   ISBN 0-472-06383-9
(pbk. : alk. paper)
    I. Reidel, James.   II. Title.   III. Series.
PS3521.E285A6   1988
814'.52—dc19   88-14295
                                                                          CIP

For Fritz Bultman

Contents

Introduction
Howard Nemerov

Memory, mine anyhow, is like the film in an old-fashioned
projector (a memory, this, from childhood), slipping its
sprockets, burning when stopped, flapping off the spool in a
cascade of imageless images just at the end, and leaving, in-
deed, nothing but a few blurred frames isolated from the
flow.

My wife and I first met Weldon and Ann Kees some while
after I got out of the Army Air Force in late summer of 1945,
over forty years ago; no recollection of how, where, when. We
were living in a freshly bedizened slum apartment building
on Twenty-fifth Street in Manhattan—the words "rehabbing"
and "gentrification" did not yet exist and anyhow would not
have applied—and were able to tell the Keeses of a vacant
apartment in the building, which they moved into. In return,
Weldon got me a job interview with Paramount News. They
didn't much like the apartment, and I didn't get the job.

But we were fairly close during 1945 to 1946, 'til I got a
teaching job upstate and moved away, and again during the
summer of 1949 when we all happened to be in Provincetown
and Weldon, apart from organizing a species of art-music-
poetry seminars called Forum 49, introduced us to such
friends, mostly painters, as Adolph Gottlieb, Hans Hoff-
mann, William Baziotes, Fritz Bultman, Franz Kline, the poet
Cecil Hemley . . . but all this had to be confirmed from books,
for memory retains nothing of it but an afternoon at Gott-
lieb's and a rather foolish evening at the Forum where I read
my poesies and other people said, or did, this that and the
other.

We were friends, though, and kept up by correspondence while I was first at Hamilton College and then at Bennington, and even after Weldon and Ann moved to California on a drive across the country which he called, even after memorializing rather fondly many of its place-names, "the space between two oceans." Weldon was always a sweeping man with a phrase.

When I looked for this fairly steady correspondence it wasn't there. I quite remember tipping one of Weldon's letters into the proof copy of his *Collected Poems*, edited by Donald Justice—which, irresponsible as I seem from this account, I really did review—but when I made a search the other day I couldn't even find his *Collected Poems*. And when I asked for letters of Weldon's from Olin Library's Special Collections at Washington University where I teach, no one could find any. So I am, if by carelessness and mischance, in the condition of that friend of The Hero in one of Auden's poems,

> who answered some
> Of his long marvelous letters, but kept none.

Save that I answered all of them, I always do. And they were both long and marvelous, crisp, sardonic, full of gossip (especially about people I never knew, or knew but slightly), and thoroughly characteristic.

(The reader should reflect here that when we are young we have no anticipation that every written word will be dissertation-meat, that we should save our bar bills, laundry lists, other lists—I had one that began promisingly "Kool-pop, pickles, gin," and wish I knew how *that* went on—and, most of all, the letters of all those friends who were going to be famous enough to be subjects of study by scholars and critics.)

Weldon was six years my senior, and senior to my friends, when we got home from the war and Reed Whittemore revived the magazine *Furioso*, which he had started with James Angleton while they were still undergraduates at Yale; worth mentioning here because Weldon, though not an editor, was an associate of and contributor to the magazine and had his book *The Fall of the Magicians* chosen as a selection of the

Furioso Book Club, which means that there may be a couple of hundred copies, together with about the same number of my first book *The Image and the Law*, still in an attic in Northfield, Minnesota, where Reed was living at the time.

He was older than we were, and wiser in his generation. He may have lived low on the hog, but, as Stanley Elkin has said in another connection, at least he was on the hog. He had a job, he had jobs, he knew people who if they didn't count then were going to count later.

And now, if he did indeed die by going off the Golden Gate Bridge on July 18, 1955, I am decades older than he got to be. His body was never found, only his car left at the entry ramp, and speculation elevating itself to legend said that he had gone to Mexico; a poem added later that he had found a sixteen-year-old mistress there.* In that event, he would still be senior to me by half a dozen years, and aged seventy-three, as well as the hero of such myth as attached itself to, e.g., Arthur, Barbarossa, Hitler. Chief argument against that is that no one who knew Weldon Kees could imagine him keeping silent for three decades.

For it was as much as anything by his talk that I remember him. Quiet, anecdotal, drawling in delivery so as to sharpen the epigrammatic point at the end, he yet gave an impression of utter seriousness, combining in the best proportions to interest his then young hearers, ferocious idealism, knowing cynicism, and that mastery of the incongruous that makes wit work.

Weldon was certainly as vast and various a talent as it has ever been my luck to know. Among his many gifts, the one for verse should probably come first, and has been amply attested to by other writers as well as by myself. But he was also accomplished in painting, well enough certainly to have exhibited in the company of many who later became famous; he was both composer and performer at jazz piano; skilled at making movies and at still photography as well; able to collaborate with Jurgen Ruesch on a book (for which he did most of the photographs) on nonverbal communication; and, last, as

---

*"Weldon Kees in Mexico, 1965" by David Wojahn.—ED.

critic, intellectual, and social historian, in which capacity he appears in this collection.

The pieces gathered here are of interest first off because of their author, a brilliant and various and always interested intelligence; second, maybe, as showing how such an intelligence earned its bread in the war years and just after by writing for, e.g., *Time*, the *New York Times Book Review*, the *Nation*, about literature, art, music; before, that is, the universities offered a relative security, not highly paid, to those who cared to take it, which Weldon didn't and probably wouldn't.

These reviews and essays are also valuable as indicating the immense range not only of interests but also of authority open to Weldon Kees even as a relatively young man. As Alfred Kazin remembers him from 1942, "He was unbelievably well informed on the smallest details of modernist literature, eagerly presented himself as a walking encyclopedia on every little magazine ever published between Reykjavík and Pinsk. He was a poet who desperately wanted to be famous, to be 'up there,' as he used to say, with Eliot, Pound, and other stars in our firmament."

What happened? I don't know, and those who were closer to him don't seem to have known either. Weldon's was a life and a death, a disappearance at the least, that gives rather than lends itself to literature; a last meeting with two friends sounds, with only a little excuse from "real life," very like Proust's episode in which Swann confides in Oriane the news of his mortal illness while the Duc impatiently wants her to change her shoes for the party.

Well, thirty years later I'm still sorry to miss his sardonic and teasing voice.

BIBLIOGRAPHIC NOTE

Alfred Kazin's observations come from *Six Decades at Yaddo* (1986). Readers interested in a fuller account of the life and presumed death of Weldon Kees should consult two splendidly studied and edited books: *Weldon Kees and the Midcentury Generation: Letters, 1935–1955*, edited with an illuminating linkage of commentary by Robert E. Knoll (Lincoln: University of Nebraska Press, 1986); and *Weldon Kees: A Critical Intro-duction*, edited by Jim Elledge (Methuen, N.J.: Scarecrow Press, 1985). A 1979 issue of the magazine *Sequoia* (Stanford University) addressed the question "Is Weldon Kees America's greatest forgotten poet?" The question mark may seem to fall short of the full commitment, and it might be better to be remembered as "forgotten greatest poet"; in any event, much of the contents was absorbed into Elledge's *Critical Introduction*.

I

Juvenilia & Criterion, 1936–43

Main Street

Among present-day short story writers George Milburn has been one of the few whose work has been consistently good. If he has written nothing that has been so widely acclaimed as "The Killers" or "That Evening Sun Go Down" or "The Golden Honeymoon," he has at least done no fourth-rate pieces for the *Saturday Evening Post* or *Esquire*. His method has been mainly an extension of Ring Lardner's: an emphasis on common speech patterns, a satirical view of his people, a capacity for sustained contempt.

Milburn's *Catalogue* is a novel—that is, if you want to believe his publishers. The fault of the book is not that it isn't a novel, or that it isn't a book of short sketches; rather, the difficulty seems to be that Milburn was never quite sure of what he was doing. Several years ago he began writing sketches and stories about mail-order catalogues, and a number of these appeared in various magazines. They were complete in themselves, and could stand up with any of his earlier pieces. And the idea seemed to be a good one: Why not put all of these things together, tie them up, have a novel?

The trouble with this was that Milburn's method didn't fit into the plan. In almost everything he had written the effectiveness was dependent upon an ironic twist that gave point to what were essentially anecdotes. And in *Catalogue* the pattern had to be changed; here there is a story with that ironic twist, then a little more left dangling to be taken up later, then a quick jump to another situation and the process repeated.

Review of *Catalogue* by George Milburn, *Midwest* 1 (November, 1936).

And so the book in its entirety is not so biting and forceful as some of his earlier stories, "Sugar Be Sweet" or "A Student in Economics" or "A Pretty Cute Little Stunt." Such thick-coming irony seems strained and unconvincing; too much happens that is pointed and entirely relevant to plot, too little that is creditably pointless and lifelike.

George Milburn's ability for recording the impact of our $2.98 culture upon small town characters is so real that individual sequences are far more memorable than the book itself. Waldo Ledbetter's difficulties with his 160C3030 Speed Model Bicycle; the lynching of the innocent Negro, Sylvester Merrick; the bewilderment of Mrs. C. H. "Spike" Callahan, the taxi driver's wife, with her diseased baby—these are not quickly forgotten. And few short pieces of writing contain such Rabelaisian humor as Milburn's description of small town loafers discussing the sanitary facilities in W. S. Winston's home. His dialogue, his use of letters and signs and advertisements, above all his names—Danziger, Ira Pirtle, Herman Gutterman, Eagle Catoosa—are always right. If *Catalogue* is not Milburn at his very best, it is certainly a book to be read and enjoyed. He seems to be one of those rare writers, incapable of doing anything actually bad.

Farrell's Literary Criticism

James T. Farrell showed with the completion of his trilogy, *Studs Lonigan,* that as a novelist he possesses most of the qualities a writer should have: a sense of values, a sense of history, an ability to see into the motives of his people, an ability to create passages of unforgettable power, a memory that revealed itself through the endlessly fascinating story of the decay of a man and a society. On the heels of his success as a novelist, Farrell has produced another work that reveals him as a critic of importance; though an angry critic, lashing out at the trends he despises, pulling no punches.

Farrell's book is an answer to the sectarian sort of "leftism" that has been frequent in literary criticism for some time. Sectarianism is probably unavoidable during a period of economic upheaval, but the impact of hastily digested theories on some critics of the political Left was so strongly felt that many lost what little integrity they had, and came out with statements on literature that were breathtaking in their stupidity. There was enough nonsense published in the name of criticism to fill volume after volume. Some critics went so far as to view the function of literature and political economy as the same: the immediate use-value of a piece of work was construed to be of more importance than its aesthetic value; expressions such as "proletarian" and "bourgeois" were employed as terms of criticism, rather than as descriptive ones;

Review of *A Note on Literary Criticism* by James T. Farrell, *Prairie Schooner* 10 (Fall 1936).

bickering, log-rolling, and dogma were in many cases substituted for intelligence and honesty.

Such a carefully conceived and sensitively executed novel as Alvah C. Bessie's *Dwell in the Wilderness,* for instance, was damned as "defeatistic," in spite of the fact that it concerned the decay of the middle class, and as such should have been entitled to left-wingers' praise; while on the other hand, Robert Briffault's *Europa,* the style of which eclipsed even the manner of Thomas Wolfe and George Santayana in turgidity and clumsiness, and whose characters possessed all the reality of those in a Metro-Goldwyn-Mayer run-of-the-mill, was given the critical laurels usually accorded only Harper prize novels by the *New York Times* and female reviewers for hinterland Wednesday afternoon clubs.

Mr. Farrell is definitely on the side of sense. It should be said, however, that errors of judgment crop out that seem to have their origin in personal prejudices. An example of this is found in his lack of respect for the "collective" novel, and his insistence that a work dealing with a single principal character is, for reasons not quite clear, of a higher artistic order. Inasmuch as Farrell himself has proceeded along the path of the so-called individualistic novel, it may be assumed that he feels the need of defending his own method. His method needs no defense. It is unfortunate that he attacks the "collective" novel in this manner: the good work of such writers as Jules Romains, John Dos Passos, and Josephine Herbst, as well as others, is all in this highly effective manner.

Such mistakes as this and others—Farrell at some points does not seem to be sure of his terms—do not mar noticeably the essential soundness of his arguments. A school of writers, internationalist, its members drawn together in spite of differences of language, nationality or race, and which numbers among its ranks such men as Gide, Rolland, Gorki, Aldous Huxley, Dos Passos, and practically all of the better younger writers of all countries, needs no apologists for the body of its creative writing. Much of the criticism, however, has not been distinguished for its sense.

Farrell's book should do much to remedy this situation. It ought to receive the wide reading that is usually accorded only to William Lyon Phelps or Isabel Paterson. But probably the Phelps and Paterson customers are well-satisfied where they are. Farrell's book will go to a quite different kind of audience.

"You Want to Read It Anyway"

When the darkhaired fellow came into the place, the light-haired one was already there sitting in a booth near the back drinking a bottle of Budweiser.

"Sorry I'm late," he said.

"It's all right," the lighthaired one said.

"What held you up?"

"I was finishing Fuchs's book."

"You couldn't put it down, huh?"

"That's right," the darkhaired one said. He looked up at the waitress, who was wiping off the top of the table with a damp cloth. "Bring me one of those," he said, pointing to the bottle of beer.

They watched her as she went behind the counter.

"Well, what do you think of it now that you've finished it?" the lighthaired one asked.

"I don't know," the darkhaired one said. "I feel kind of too bad about it. It's the card-stacking I don't like, I guess."

"The card-stacking?"

"Yeh. In the book before this one, *Homage to Blenholt*, well, there he knew just what he was doing, and the book was absolutely right. Now it isn't enough for him to know just what he's doing; he has to stack the cards."

"Yeh?" the lighthaired one said. "You know, I liked *Homage to Blenholt*. It was all right."

"But in this one, this *Low Company*, you get that too-slick planning behind it, you feel that the whole thing is too well

---

Review of *Low Company* by Daniel Fuchs, *Hinterland* 1 (1937).

arranged, that the author worked the whole thing out with a slide-rule, and when you're through with it, well, you can't help feeling that it's more than a little phoney."

"I'm sorry to hear that," the lighthaired one said. "Fuchs is a good man."

"Sure," the darkhaired one said. "I know it. That's the hell of it."

He watched the waitress as she put the bottle down in front of him. He paid her and drank a little of the beer.

"This one's laid in Coney Island, which Fuchs calls Neptune Beach. In a joint there—a soda fountain–confectionery —he assembles a lot of swell characters. Incidentally, the man can handle self-pity as well as anyone I know of. Anyway, there's Spitzbergen, who runs the place; and Shubunka, a great shambling man who runs a string of cathouses; and a sodajerk named Shorty who spends most of his time dreaming of women; and a naive kid named, lessee, what was his name, oh yes, Arthur. Arthur's his name. And a gambler named Karty; Fuchs had a character something like Karty in the other book."

"And what happens?" the lighthaired one asked.

"Oh, they're all frustrated, beaten, killed or maimed or defeated in one way or another, and that's where the cardstacking comes in. I wish he wouldn't do that. I wish he'd take it easy. A writer can get into a lot of trouble being more interested in working things out than in the way they would work out."

"I'll have to get hold of it."

"Yes, you want to read it," the darkhaired one said. "You want to read it anyway. Everything considered. They're some fine things in it."

"But it isn't any *Homage to Blenholt,* eh?" the lighthaired one asked.

"Nope, it isn't any *Homage to Blenholt,*" the darkhaired one said. "That's the trouble."

"Have a cigarette?" the lighthaired one said.

Fifth Caravan

This is the fifth of the Caravan volumes, and the first to appear since 1931. Confronted with a book of nearly seven hundred pages, which contains five novelettes, eight stories, three essays, extracts from novels and plays, letters, many poems, two poetic plays, and a novel by Paul Horgan, one longs to be Mr. Edward J. O'Brien for at least a short while. A few stars scattered here and there and you have the whole book covered, nothing is omitted, maybe you've formed a nice pattern of asterisks,* everybody's name is mentioned. But barring that, you can at least have a Roll of Honor, another favorite O'Brien device.

First place among the contributors easily goes to Ernest Brace for his story, "Sound of Trumpets," a study of a man and his wife torn apart by the differences in their political beliefs. Unlike a number of the writers in this *Caravan*, Mr. Brace knows exactly how to push the reader into the realm of living people and keep him there, believing every bit of it, never questioning. Mr. Brace doesn't, like Bessie Breuer in "The Dinner Party," bore you to death with warmed-over Tess Slesinger *cum* the last forty-five pages of *Ulysses;* or, like Sherwood Anderson, in his unconvincing tale of still another

---

Review of *The New Caravan* edited by Alfred Kreymborg, Lewis Mumford, and Paul Rosenfeld, *Midwest* 1 (January, 1937).

*Kees refers to a system of one to four asterisks for rating distinguished fiction used by the editor of the *Best Short Stories* series, Edward J. O'Brien.—ED.

Chicago grotesque in the advertising business, send you running back to *Winesburg, Ohio,* to reassure yourself that once upon a time Anderson deserved all those genuflections. And easily ranking with Brace is Richard Wright, a young Negro whose material in "Big Boy Leaves Home" has been the common property of Southern writers for years. Yet Wright's gift for dialogue infuses his story of a brutal lynching with much new meaning, and the terrible situation that has been dealt with so often is here clearer, sharper, and closer. His Negroes' speech is as accurate as any that has been written.

There is much of the same feeling of chaos in Meridel LeSueur's novelette, "The Bird," with its overtones of decay and horror, and its central character, a boy, mingling with the hopeless passengers of an old ship. Bob Brown's story of a Louisiana county fair is actually a fine piece of reporting; his fair is an exploited, exploiting world in miniature, accurately observed and described. On the Roll of Honor goes Raymond Holden's "Animal Vegetable . . . ," which has a lean irony not found elsewhere in the volume. And I would include the extract from Eugene Joffe's novel, "Month Before Last," even though it is badly marred by a passage in which Mr. Joffe unfortunately tries the stream-of-consciousness method on the mind of a small baby. The baby sounds too much like a combination of Thomas Wolfe and William Faulkner for anyone's comfort. "There Was No Time," a fragment from the late Eva Goldbeck's autobiography, is, as Lewis Mumford has written in a note: ". . . more penetrating, more discriminating, more rigorous, more justly appreciative than one either a critic or a friend could write."

There is an interesting experimental play in verse by a new writer, Delmore Schwartz, and Emmjo Basshe's poetic play, "The Dream of the Dollar," as well as many poems by Wallace Stevens, Witter Bynner, Conrad Aiken, Phelps Putnam, Stanley Burnshaw, Muriel Rukeyser, and others. Much of the verse is over-intellectualized, and for this reason the work of Howard Nutt, Ruth Lechlitner, and Reuel Denney stands out in its simplicity. You will also find William Carlos Williams managing to be pretty boring in his play in verse about Washington, and E. E. Cummings asking you to follow his example and stop thinking.

I find I've managed to name only about half the contributors to *The New Caravan*. Perhaps that one-star, two-star, three-star idea wasn't such a bad one after all.

You Wouldn't Catch Hemingway
Letting Anyone Go Downstairs
with a Humble Eagerness

In *Now That April's Here* Morley Callaghan seems to be interested in why people are sad, or, more particularly, why they happen to be sad as the result of situations that are becoming somewhat formularized for him. *People Are Sad* would be a more revealing title than the one he has selected: most of the characters in these numerous stories wind up in the last paragraph feeling "suddenly sad" about what has happened to them, whether they are young husbands and wives, or priests, or fathers, or the newspaper reporter who saw the fish thrown at the old hangman. Morley Callaghan is interested in what makes people sad (especially in the last paragraph), and rarely is he much concerned with their cruelty, banality, anger, vanity, hopefulness, their determination, or their ambition or the hundred and one other things that make human beings what they are. He seems desperately afraid sometimes that we won't get the point, that we won't believe in his people; and so he is constantly interceding, letting us know that Greg was "an opinionated, arrogant man" with "a natural fierceness in his nature," or that Frank had a "laconic, straightforward manner." In addition to feeling "suddenly sad" in the last paragraph or so, people have "surges of joy," feel in themselves "a strange excitement," or

Review of *Now That April's Here* by Morley Callaghan and *O. Henry Memorial Prize Stories* edited by Harry Hansen, *Prairie Schooner* 11 (Spring 1937).

"a vast uneasiness." (All of these quotations came from one story, just so you don't think I'm hunting around for this sort of thing.)

Although Callaghan is entirely capable of showing characters through their actions, and does this on occasion with a good deal of his early skill, more and more he is depending on abstractions for his effects, and with a considerable loss in artistry. Callaghan's irony, which was more apparent in his earlier stories—I remember particularly his remarkable little sketch about the drunk who wandered into a confessional booth and asked to be let off at Yonge Street—has gone to seed, and in its place has been substituted his tedious pity. It has been pointed out somewhere that Callaghan is entirely free of the influence of Hemingway, whom Callaghan was accused of imitating. A little more of Hemingway's influence would be a fine thing for Callaghan in these days when he writes of a man going downstairs with "a humble eagerness." You wouldn't catch Hemingway letting anyone go downstairs with a humble eagerness.

Since the high priestess of the punch ending, Blanche Colton Williams, has been missing as editor of the O. Henry Award volumes, there has been a greater evenness apparent in the selections. This year is no exception. Nancy Hale and two university professors have chosen the stories, almost all of which are capably turned out, stories by Faulkner, James Gould Cozzens (first prize with a *Saturday Evening Post* story), Virginia Bird, Walter D. Edmonds, Paul Horgan, Ernest Brace, and others. The only piece that makes much of a contribution is William March's ironic sketch of the traveling men who found the scrap of paper in a hotel room.

While the O'Brien [*Best Short Stories*] volumes usually offer something startling, and at least represent a base for some worthwhile controversy, the dead level of merit in the O. Henry anthologies rarely excites much more interest than the discovery of a new genius by one of the book clubs. I wish some enterprising anthologist would come along and reprint some things by some of these writers: D. A. Davidson, John Cheever, Charles Bradford, Eudora Welty, Fred R. Miller, Hilde Abel, and Robert O. Erisman. These, along with a few others, are doing some of the most interesting short stories appearing today, and aside from Miller, I don't believe any of them have had work reprinted in books. There's still a lot of spade work to be done, and I can't think of a better time to do it than right now.

Repeating a Lot of
Dreiser's Mistakes

This is Farrell's ninth book to be published, and his third book of short stories. As they continue to appear with regularity, it becomes clear that Farrell is building a world of his own: everything that he writes fits into one large work, and in this respect he resembles such writers as Proust, Balzac, and Jules Romains. As yet, however, Farrell's disgust for many aspects of our civilization is so great that he stays within a somewhat narrow orbit of human experience: in the present volume of stories, for instance, the same note of loathing is sounded again and again until it becomes monotonous. This is not true of his novels: in them he permits himself to write long flat passages which give balance to an alarmingly accurate vision of a decaying society.

In a note of explanation to his work which was printed in the *New Quarterly* several years ago, Farrell emphasized the point that there is a great dichotomy between literature and direct experience, implying that he resorted to devices to remedy this breach. He also wrote that he was not content to "megaphone stereotypes." It seems now that in his short stories at least he is setting up a different sort of dichotomy, one in which his own vision of evil is more static than life itself. And this comes dangerously close to megaphoning stereotypes.

There is also too much sloppy writing: almost every story

Review of *Can All This Grandeur Perish?* by James T. Farrell, *Prairie Schooner* 11 (Summer 1937).

begins with a physical description of the main character, unpleasantly reminiscent of the worst of prewar writing; there are too many adverbs; there is far too much that shows haste and thoughtlessness.

Farrell, as has been said time after time, is one of our really important writers—probably the most important since Dreiser. But that doesn't mean that he has to repeat a lot of Dreiser's mistakes, or think up new ones all his own.

Successors to the Old *Dial, Pagany,* and *Windsor Quarterly*

Here are three books, all of which emphasize experimental writing. Taken together, they give a good idea of the directions in which a large group of the younger writers are moving, and supply some indication of which way the wind is blowing. For a great majority of these writers, most of whom began to write during the depression years, it blows Left. But there is little work in any of the three volumes that shows the influence of hastily digested political views; there is surprisingly little of the empty sloganizing that was so predominant in the "proletarian" literature of the early thirties. As William Phillips and Philip Rahv point out in their essay, "Literature in a Political Decade," in *New Letters,* "The more conscious craftsmen in fiction and poetry would not surrender themselves to the . . . new aesthetic code . . . of Granville Hicks and Michael Gold." At least two of the books—*New Letters* and *365 Days*—are fascinating in their plan and scope, and all three of them contain at least some work of more than ephemeral interest.

Paradoxically, the book that is most "advanced" contains the least work of any real body. Kay Boyle must have thought she had struck upon something pretty breathtaking when the idea came to her: to line up all the writers she could think of and set them to concocting little three-hundred-word

Review of *365 Days* edited by Kay Boyle and others; *American Stuff* by members of the Federal Writers' Project; and *New Letters in America* edited by Horace Gregory, *Prairie Schooner* 11 (Winter 1937).

sketches, each based upon some event in the year 1934. A number of the writers stayed away from news events—Miss Boyle's pet scheme—and the way it turned out, that wasn't such a bad idea. Out of these 365 sketches, some of which are very badly done indeed, only a few remain memorable, and many of these are by well established writers. I recall especially those by William March, Grace Flandrau, and James T. Farrell. But the book as a whole is a collection of minor scraps and will no doubt be remembered chiefly as a literary curiosity. That Miss Boyle sought to give encouragement to the sketch is a heartening thing; too few are written, probably because of the difficulty involved in getting them published; but the next time, it would be a good idea if she took her time and made her selections more judiciously.

American Stuff attempts to give some picture of the type of writing being done by those employed by the Federal Writers' Project, Works Progress Administration, when they are not trying, at one and the same time, to write honest histories and guidebooks and to keep from annoying Chambers of Commerce and local patriots. Evidently, when the call went out for material for this anthology, most of the writers felt, with reason, that it would be just another one of those minor Government projects that come to nothing; and so we get an introduction to the volume by Project Director Alsberg, apologizing somewhat lamely for the book's uneven quality. After one has read Richard Wright's excellent autobiographical sketches on what it means to be a Negro in the South, Fred Rothernell's piece about a girl who buys a big dinner to forget that she is on relief, the poetry of Kenneth Rexroth, and the stories by Leon Dorais and Jerre Mangione, there isn't much left. The book also contains a great deal of folklore material that has been better presented elsewhere, and an evidently trunk-worn story by Vardis Fisher. The book is illustrated by members of the Federal Art Project. These help an anthology that could have been so much better when one considers the numerous talented persons employed at one time or another by the Writers' Project.

It is obvious that Horace Gregory wanted to do something for contemporary American literature similar to that which has been done in England by John Lehman with his *New Writing*. Gregory has even gone so far as to borrow some pieces from the British books; there is work by W. H. Auden, Robert Herring, and John Hampson. There are also translations from continental literature: a brief sketch by Louis Guilloux and a story by Franz Kafka. Out of some forty contributions, Eugene Joffe's story is easily the best. The promise that Gregory gives in his excellent introduction is not fulfilled by the work included, even with names like Frederic Prokosch, John Cheever, and Robert Fitzgerald. Gregory seems to want more emphasis on the "fable," and less on straight naturalistic writing. It appears that he wasn't able to find much of this: Auden's three pages are good; so is I. J. Kapstein's "The Man in the Jail Is Not Jesus," but that isn't enough.

It may be that these books are more important in indicating a publishing change than in the material they offer. Little magazines have folded so rapidly during the last few years that it was necessary for something to take their place or allow much good work to remain unpublished. Such anthologies or yearbooks as *New Letters,* which is promised every six months, the British *New Writing,* three issues of which have already appeared, and the annual *New Directions,* are the successors to the old *Dial, Pagany,* and *Windsor Quarterly.* The main difference: these cost more, and there hasn't been much improvement in editing.

New Directions 1937

Writing of an experimental nature makes up its own rules as
it goes along, but the finished work usually runs the risk of
being judged by rules that are not at all new. What finally
determines the quality of any piece of writing rests upon what
light it sheds on the phases of doing and being; in short, the
old stuff: characterization, mood, movement, etc. Although
Mr. T. S. Eliot expects the "serious" reader to go over difficult
works six or seven times, taking "at least as much trouble as a
barrister reading an important decision on a complicated
case," the best experimental work usually reveals most of its
worth in a first reading. To insist upon such serious attention
and study is to relegate literature to a leisure class minority
activity that ends in pointless philological investigations or
worse. It is a commonplace of our time that on one hand our
mass reading sinks lower and lower (both in style and matter),
while the "new writing" veers more and more toward private
concerns and unintelligibility. About the only point of re-
semblance between the sadomasochist pulp literature flood-
ing the newsstands and a work of the nature of, say, St. J.
Perse's *Anabasis* or Joyce's *Anna Livia Plurabelle*, is the use of
words as tools.

The work in *New Directions 1937* is very unevenly selected,
but at that it is by far the most exciting of the volumes which it
closely resembles, *New Letters, New Writing, American Caravan,*
etc. Three selections, Cocteau's play *Les Mariés de la Tour Eiffel,*

Review of *New Directions 1937* edited by James Laughlin IV, *Prai-
rie Schooner* 12 (Spring 1938).

Henry Miller's "Walking Up and Down in China," and Delmore Schwartz's short story "The Commencement Day Address," would distinguish any volume. Aside from the very real skill of all these men with words, I think much of the success of their work arises from a sense of *rapport* which they immediately establish with the reader: one knows what they're talking about. One knows that Cocteau is satirizing, among other things, bourgeois marriage; knows Miller's mood (Joyce plus Thomas Wolfe); knows the terror in back of Schwartz's magnificent story (which, along with Eudora Welty's "Flowers for Marjorie,"—*Prairie Schooner,* 1937—is about the most perfect and disturbing story published this year).

There is other work of value by E. E. Cummings, William Carlos Williams, and William Saroyan, and a generally sound article on language and meaning by James Laughlin IV, the volume's editor. But Kenneth Rexroth, often an interesting poet, is lost in a fog of private sources (I would guess Whitehead, chiefly); so are most of the others. Still others are merely dull. There are also dreams. And last of all, there is a play by Gertrude Stein, which is highly recommended for its tiresome humor and for its value as a soporific.

Three Books

One way of judging a writer—if you are interested in one-way judgments, as a lot of critics seem to be these days—is on the basis of how much he keeps himself out of the picture. Saroyan is like looking for escape in a short beer. He's all over the place, though not quite so emancipated as in his previous volumes. *Love, Here Is My Hat* has fewer of those windy, soul-lost pages of rhapsodical writing that had the critics tossing the word "genius" around; consequently, a little "rich" writing, and stories of scarcely any weight to speak of. All in all, a poor book, with possibly one good story. Maybe it was Hollywood; maybe it was the Packard (or was it a Cadillac?) that Saroyan bought and has his picture taken in, smiling gaily; perhaps other things we don't know about. But it's my none-too-original guess that it's Saroyan's flair for being able to grind them out in wholesale lots, and letting the stories fall where they may.

The publication of James T. Farrell's collected stories brings out forcefully the narrowness of this powerful novelist's range of vision when he limits himself to the short form. In describing the writer of burlesque, Kenneth Burke has written: "[He] makes no attempt to get inside the psyche of his victim. Instead, he is content to select the externals of behavior, and drive them to a logical conclusion" that becomes their "reduction to absurdity." By program, he obliter-

Review of *Love, Here Is My Hat* by William Saroyan; *The Short Stories of James T. Farrell;* and *Life Along the Passaic River* by William Carlos Williams, *Rocky Mountain Review* 3 (Winter 1938–39).

ates his victim's discriminations. He is "heartless." He converts every "perhaps" into a "positively." He deliberately suppresses any consideration of the "mitigating circumstances" that would put his subject in a better light. If the victim performs an act that would appear well when done slowly, he performs the same act at top speed; if the act is more appropriate for speed, he portrays it in slow motion. Hilariously, he converts a manner into a mannerism. The method of burlesque (polemic, caricature) is partial not only in the sense of partisan, but also in the "sense of incompleteness." I have no idea whom Burke had in mind; but, as far as his short stories are concerned, and to a lesser extent in his novels, this fits Mr. Farrell perfectly. There is much truth in these ugly pictures of South Side Chicago life, but it is certainly much less than the whole truth, and closer to Swift, Céline, Lardner, and Henry Miller, than to many of the writers to whom Farrell has mistakenly been compared.

As for William Carlos Williams's *Life Along the Passaic River*, I truly believe it to be one of the most interesting and exciting books of short stories that has appeared in America in years, a book to put beside Hemingway's *In Our Time* and Katherine Anne Porter's *Flowering Judas*. For thirty years Dr. Williams has been writing, perfecting his style, working in semi-obscurity, his only outlets those of experimental magazines and books of limited circulation. He has done this without surrendering to obscurity, defeatism, sentimentality, or compromise, factors that have been responsible for the deaths of more promising writers than one would care to mention. In the face of indifference on the part of commercial publishers and the general reading public, he has produced numerous fine poems; a novel of great merit, *White Mule;* and at least three other books of worth. At his best, as he is in this volume of stories, Dr. Williams is quite simply the finest craftsman writing prose in America today.

Four Poets

Mr. John Russell McCarthy's *Five Times the World,* according
to the foreword, is "the story of a boy and a girl who live, with
their small tribe, near the big trees. The time is perhaps fif-
teen thousand years from today." The dedication reads: "To
————," making it possible for one to insert any name one
might like. My own copy was fixed up to read: *To Robert Frost,
il miglior fabbro.* The volume should hold no terrors for those
who feel kindly toward Mr. Frost's work; and one who has
prepared himself for Mr. McCarthy through Mr. Frost is un-
likely to experience shock when he comes upon these lines:

> Jon and his fellows took the high trail
> that circled the temple grounds, passed the huts
> and stockade where the first-born of all women
> were kept sacredly apart awaiting their divine
> mission. Hi and Wil stepped close to the pen
> but were silent; speech with the sacred children
> was tabu. Jon kept aloof.

I think we all feel Jon did the right thing. As for Hi and Wil, I
am not so sure.

Mr. Howard Nutt is satirical, brash, intolerant, E-c-o-n-o-
m-i-c, uneven, and a more than part-time member of what we
will call the Cult of the Superfluous Exclamation Point.
(Blackmurish, I noted forty-two of them in a hurried count of

Review of *Five Times the World* by John Russell McCarthy; *Special
Laughter* by Howard Nutt; *New Journey* by Sydney Salt; and *In Plato's
Garden* by Lincoln Fitzell, *Fantasy* 7 (1939).

twenty-five poems.) He admires words like "pious-puckered," "spine-spiked," "soulseining," "woman-wisdom," "boodle-bore," "penwhispering"; he doesn't like "antisocial" poets. Most of his work, now collected in *Special Laughter*, is sicklied o'er with the pink cast of the late United Front, a period during which an amazingly large quantity of verse was written, apparently, to let poets' friends know that they were frequenting acceptable political pastures. This was serious business in that weird time; unfortunately, not much poetry came out of it; read now, a good deal of the period's "social" verse calls up a vision of Mr. Granville Hicks hovering near and shaking a warning finger.

Mr. Nutt's verses, read in magazines during the thirties, sounded better than they do now; they date considerably. His contemptuousness is far up the road, nearly out of sight; his talent—a bizarre, eclectic figure we seem to have come upon before, who tenders cards that read "ELIOT," "CUMMINGS," "FEARING"—describes a circle some three miles back.

Eliot-Nutt:

> The gaiety of desperation coughs
> Three last queer piccolo notes,
> And they, too, wander off
> To alienate themselves among
> The bricks and ventpipes of the commonplace.
>
> The moon has no expression on its face.

Cummings-Nutt:

> Whobody lay three blankets hot
> In blue afterism.
> Because he had no anywhat
> To ransom protoplasm.

Fearing-Nutt:

> Don't look now, but—
> WHO'S THAT MAN? . . .
> Bernard, the famous bathroom bard,
> Actor Hector, breathing hard,

> The bishop's bastard son, who drinks,
> The home town girl who got made good . . .

Yet he can write good poetry; "The Little Deaths," which I would like to quote if there were space, seems to me a very good poem indeed. More work of its quality would be most welcome. Up to now, Mr. Nutt's laughter is bitter and raucous, but not, I am afraid, so very special.

Mr. Sydney Salt has a crush on the discoverer of America: a previous volume of his was called *Christopher Columbus,* and his *New Journey* is a long poem celebrating the Italian navigator. It seems to rely heavily on Columbus's log and letters, even including correspondence exchanged between Columbus and Gorricio. The poem is diffuse and lacking in intensity, which Mr. Salt tries to make up for through a liberal use of the exclamation points left over by Mr. Nutt. *New Journey* is in the tradition, I suppose, of *Anabase, Journey of the Magi,* and *Conquistador,* but scarcely of that company. When Mr. Salt writes

> Gaspar, you are patient and dear,
> you are a man of Christ,
> and by that quick token are saved—
> how happy happy happy you are!

and adds

> The men are without hope.

one sympathizes with them and understands.

Mr. Lincoln Fitzell confesses to a high regard for the poetic convictions of Yvor Winters, lives close to the source of the California classicism, and won the Shelley Memorial Award in 1937. *In Plato's Garden* is a collection covering eleven years of his work. Unpossessed by the high moral fever associated with Mr. Winters's group, Mr. Fitzell is no deviationist, however, when it comes to emulating their technical procedure: he sticks close to four-line stanzas of iambic tetrameter. This, combined with a rather uninteresting vocabulary, not much to say, and an ear that is quite bad, results in verse that grows quickly monotonous; most often he sounds like Winters, sometimes like Housman, and, sometimes like the late Wm. Vaughn Moody. Mr. Fitzell is fond of such expressions as "manly will," "rash youth," and "earth-mumbled woe." The book is beautifully printed and bound.

A Katherine Anne Porter Legend

A Katherine Anne Porter legend has developed—a legend of the trunks she takes with her from place to place that are supposedly filled with unfinished manuscripts; of residences in the old South, Denver, New York, Mexico City, Berlin, Paris, Bermuda, Majorca, Baton Rouge; of her experiences writing for various revolutionary organizations in Mexico; of her marriages, her beauty, her unfinished novel, *Many Redeemers,* promised for years; of the uncompleted study of Cotton Mather, announced eleven years ago and never published; of her acquaintanceship with Hart Crane. But the most important fact about Miss Porter is the meagerness of her output; for years her reputation has been based on a book of short stories, *Flowering Judas,* ten stories of great depth, humor, and understanding. She is less productive than any other writer of merit one can recall; but her patience and meticulousness have resulted in work of intelligence and form.

This capacity for form is unusual among present-day American writers: only a few of them seem to possess sufficient creative and critical sense to produce with a degree of sustained excellence. One thinks of Miss Porter, Dr. Williams, Hemingway, a few others—for the rest, a series of failures and an occasional, perhaps accidental, success.

Miss Porter is an artist in the sense that James and Flaubert were artists: her material determines her method. Instead of

---

Review of *Pale Horse, Pale Rider* by Katherine Anne Porter, *Fantasy* 7 (1939).

flourishing her style, she puts it to use. Consequently she is capable of writing with breadth and variety; her style is malleable and serves the purposes demanded of it. The second edition of *Flowering Judas* was one of the richest and varied collections by an American author—rich in mood, structure, locale, and characters.

Pale Horse, Pale Rider, her first book in many years, contains three long stories, "Old Mortality," "Noon Wine," and the title story. The first is one of her finest. It displays her smoothness and her humor; every character is subtly drawn, from its hysterical, complex heroine who runs chaotically from marriage to death, to the old aunt, one of Miss Porter's most brilliant characterizations. The South of forty or fifty years ago is presented in sharp and revealing strokes, with nostalgia kept in the background. The story barely misses the stature of such works as "The Dead," "Death in Venice," and James's novelettes. In the last few pages, Miss Porter turns her attention from the persons observed to the "observer," Miranda; up to this point the attention has been solidly fixed on the former. The effect is hysterical, uncontrolled, and extremely unfortunate.

The same hysteria permeates all of "Pale Horse, Pale Rider," but it derives from its subject, the influenza epidemic of the draft days when America entered the First World War. Miranda is now the central character, working on a newspaper, in love with a young soldier whose death comes at the story's end. It is highly recommended, particularly to those who are eager to fight another "last war for Democracy." "Noon Wine" is in direct contrast to the subjectivity of the other tales. Melodramatic, ironic, the story of a harmonica-playing farmhand and a murder, it has less substance, but it is without the flaws in the other stories which apparently result from the author's too close identification of herself with Miranda.

Fearing's Collected Poems

Kenneth Fearing's first book of poems, *Angel Arms,* appeared quietly in 1929. It was not until six years later that his second volume, *Poems,* was issued by an obscure publisher. The year, 1935, was one in which the literary politicians of the Left were solidifying what seemed at the time to be their positions, before personal quarrels and the vagaries of international power politics had done away with poems in which clenched fists, noble workers and red dawns abounded (particularly in the concluding stanzas), when Fearing still found it possible to write of "millions of voices become one voice . . . millions of hands that move as one." It had taken him over ten years to write his first two books; the last two, *Dead Reckoning* and *The Agency,* were produced with somewhat more ease, apparently, in half that time. Now all four have been collected into a single volume.

Contemporary civilization has been anything but reserved in providing its satirical writers with abundant horrors; and Fearing, who gathers up-to-the-minute horrors with all the eager thoroughness of a bibliophile cackling over pagination errors, has as much cause to be grateful to civilization's provision as have Mr. Céline, Mr. Faulkner, and Mr. Henry Miller. With more anger than hate he probes the choicest exhibits: "the daughters, living but mad," Hitler and Jack the Ripper, "dreamworld Dora and hallucination Harold," the "gutters, scrapheaps, breadlines, jails."

> The child was nursed on government bonds. Cut its teeth on a
> hand grenade. Grew fat on shrapnel. Bullets. Barbed wire.
> Chlorine gas. Laughed at the bayonet through its heart.

It is a civilization of gunmen and dope addicts, madmen and the dead, "realistically" presented and remarkably like the tabloids. Fearing's horrors are rigorously prevented from assuming the tortured shapes of those neo-Surrealistic hobgoblins that, popping out at us from certain poems in increasing numbers, seldom say Boo with sufficient clarity or conviction.

The world of Fearing is nothing if not metropolitan. He is as involved in, and fascinated by, metropolitan existence (with its "touch of vomit-gas in the evening air") as Frost with his New England landscape, decorated with common-places, and Jeffers with his prop boulders and gulls. There is no relief or escape from the city, from the "profitable smile invisible above the skyscrapers," "the loud suburban heroes," "the lunch-hour boredom," "the street that sleeps and screams" where "only desire and profit are real." The occasional references to "cool valleys," "fresh green hills," and "scented air from the fields" seem almost exotic and unreal. West of New Jersey there is scarcely any world—Butte and Detroit and "the empty barns of the west" are only names, faint in the smoke of Manhattan Island. Held by this life in a futile ambivalence that has persisted for fifteen years, Fearing's mood appears to have changed little from the "fly-specked Monday evening" of *Angel Arms* to the "champagne for supper, murder for breakfast" of the most recent poems, although the tone has become increasingly harsh. In the ticker-tape, the radio, the tabloid, the pulp magazine, and the advertisement he has found an objective correlative that has never deserted him.

"The idea underlying my poetry, as well as anything I write, is that it must be exciting; otherwise it is valueless," Fearing has written. "To this end it seemed to me necessary to discard the entire bag of conventions and codes usually associated with poetry and to create instead more exciting forms which, in all cases, are based on the material being written about. Besides being exciting, I think that poetry necessarily must be understandable. Everything in this volume has been written with the intention that its meaning should disclose itself at ordinary reading tempo." Elsewhere Fearing has very conveniently supplied critics and readers with the names of those who have influenced his work: Maurice Ravel, George Grosz, Walt Whitman, and Carl Sandburg.

Far from discarding "the entire bag of conventions and codes usually associated with poetry," he has rather taken over and extended techniques of the anti-poetic common to both Whitman and Sandburg, supplementing them with more raucous tricks not unknown to the soap-boxer, the radio orator, and the sideshow barker. Principal among these are the device of repetition, esteemed also by the writer of advertising copy; and the device of listing and cataloguing. Many of his poems depend almost exclusively upon them, one of which, "X Minus X," is representative:

> Even when your friend, the radio, is still; even when her
>   dream, the magazine, is finished; even when his life, the
>   ticker, is silent; even when their destiny, the boulevard,
>   is bare;
> And after that paradise, the dance-hall, is closed; after that
>   theatre, the clinic, is dark,
>
> Still there will be your desire, and hers, and his hopes and
>   theirs,
> Your laughter, their laughter,
> Your curse and his curse, her reward and their reward, their
>   dismay and his dismay and her dismay and yours—
>
> Even when your enemy, the collector, is dead; even when
>   your counsellor, the salesman, is sleeping; even when
>   your sweetheart, the movie queen, has spoken; even
>   when your friend, the magnate, is gone.[1]

Such a poem as "Jack Knuckles Falters" makes use of the newspaper-montage treatment employed by Dos Passos in the "Newsreel" sections of *U.S.A.:*

STAGGERS WHEN HE SEES ELECTRIC CHAIR

Five days after war was declared, I was hoping for a pardon
     from the governor,
But evidently the government has forgotten its veterans in
     their moment of need.
What brought me to the chair

WILL RUMANIAN PRINCE WED AGAIN?

Tag-ends of conversation become ironic exhibits in the first "American Rhapsody":

"I killed her because she had an evil eye." "We are not
     thinking now of our own profits of course." "Nothing
     can take back from us this night." "Let me alone, you
     God damn rat." "Two rickeys." "Cash."

"Conclusion" has sections which depend on a manner of considerable antiquity:

In the flaring parks, in the taverns, in the hushed
     academies, your murmur will applaud the wisdom
     of a thousand quacks. For theirs is the kingdom.
By your sedate nod in the quiet office you will grieve
     with the magnate as he speaks of sacrifice. For
     his is the power.
Your knowing glance will affirm the shrewd virtue of
     clown and drudge; directors' room or street-corner,
     the routine killer will know your candid smile;
     your handclasp, after the speeches at the club,
     will endorse the valor of loud suburban heroes.
     For theirs is the glory, forever and ever.

In "Denouement," question after question is followed by:

Morphine. Veronal. Veronal. Morphine. Morphine.
     Morphine. Morphine.

in a way that suggests the last lines of *Sweeney Agonistes*, scarcely, however, raising one's admiration to such a pitch. Like the now famous ending of "Dirge" ("Bong, Mr., bong, Mr., bong, Mr., bong.") it is successful in a way that so many of his repetitive lines never are, with their inescapable suggestion that the poet is merely nursing along a bad habit:

Certain that each is forever doomed and lost, and
    there where he lies is forever damned, and
    damned, and damned, and damned.
                                                    ("Net")

Adjust to the present, and to a longer view.
To cities shining in the sky tonight, and smoking
    in the dust tomorrow.
Adjust the mothers. And the husbands. And the
    fathers. And the Wives.
                              ("The Doctor Will See You Now")

SAY THE LAST WORD, YOU LONG STRAIGHT
    STREETS,
SAY THE LAST WORD, YOU WISE GUY, DUMB GUY,
    SOFT GUY, RIGHT GUY, FALL GUY, TOUGH
    GUY,
SAY THE LAST WORD, YOU BLACK SKY ABOVE.
                        ("A Dollar's Worth of Blood, Please")

Although his vision of life in general, once limited largely to the vision of a *New Masses* cartoon, has broadened little, it is a tribute to his very real gifts (supplemented by a temperament chary of uplift) that within such limits he has written a number of the best poems deriving from a source that is at once narrow, born of immediacy, and stifling, and one that has fathered few poets of his sharp awareness. He is a genuine "natural," a figure rare enough at any time to be appealing. Even at the last, when his sour wit shows signs of having curdled, and when his repetitions and lists, forceful and effective in limited amounts, become tiresome and mechanical, degenerating into a facile and overwrought shrillness, there are still more than a few poems that are exactly what their author wished them to be; they are valuable and exciting.

1. *Collected Poems* is full of changes, some of which may be worth noting. The third line of this poem, for instance, has been rewritten since "X Minus X" appeared in *Poems;* the line originally was:

> Still there will be your desire, and her desire,
>   and his desire, and their desire

Other revisions are even more interesting. A line in the *Poems* version of "No Credit" read:

> the reflection goes from the mirror; as the shadow,
>   of even a Communist, is gone from the wall

It has been revised in this way:

> . . . as the shadow, of even a rebel, is gone from the wall

In "Denouement" (*Poems* version), a single phrase, "Your party lives," has become "Your brothers live." Several lines from "What If Mr. Jesse James Should Some Day Die?" catalogue the names of a number of persons, objects, and institutions the poet wished to dispense with; they appeared this way in *Poems:*

> No more breadlines. No more blackjacks. No more
>   Roosevelts. No more Hearsts.
>
> No more vag tanks, Winchells, True Stories, deputy
>   sheriffs, no more scabs.
>
> No more trueblue, patriotic, doublecross leagues.
>   No more Ku Klux Klan. No more heart-to-heart
>   shakedowns. No more D.A.R.

This passage, in the *Collected Poems,* has been given a considerable going-over:

> No more breadlines. No more blackjacks. And save
>   us from the sheriffs, the G-men and the scabs.

No more heart-to-heart shakedowns. No more Ku Klux
   Klan. No more trueblue, patriotic, doublecross
   leagues.

Recent Books

Read one after another, these three novels of Middlewestern farm life in the present century bring on the dismal feeling, in at least one reader, that here is genuine irresponsibility—not the sort that worries Mr. MacLeish so much these days—but the irresponsibility that blandly produces unbeautiful and frequently unreadable prose. Scarcely a sentence in any of these books is really "written." The late Scott Fitzgerald, who wrote one good book, once remarked, "How anyone could take up the responsibility of being a novelist without a sharp and concise attitude about life is a puzzle to me." And how much more puzzling are some of our so-called novelists whose works read like first drafts turned out under the heaviest pressure, innocent of grace or wit or form.

Mr. Corey's *The Road Returns* is, if I must split hairs, the best of these three books. It represents a compromise between the collective novel and the family chronicle of farm life, and is a rather pedestrian account of agrarian Iowa from 1917 to 1923. On the first page the farm land is "quickening in the April sun," and we are introduced to the Mantz family—at least I was introduced to them, not having read Mr. Corey's first novel, *Three Miles Square,* which detailed their pre-First-World-War adventures. They and their neighbors are carried through seven years of war, influenza, birth, death, good times and bad, mostly bad. The book bristles with

Review of *Sons of the Fathers* by Albert Halper; *The Road Returns* by Paul Corey; and *Light Sons and Dark* by David Cornel DeJong, *Accent* 1 (Spring 1941).

clichés: "pent-up resentment," "her heart warmed," "last year was still bitter in her memory," "crestfallen look," "bitter sigh," "with trembling fingers," etc. Mr. Louis Bromfield, in a fine rush to go out of his way to find a simile, has said that Mr. Corey's book is "like a painting of Pieter Breughel," a statement devised to frighten old men from the chimney seat, no doubt. But the novel is not much better, not much worse than the run of farm novels. (Bobbs-Merrill have given it one of the ugliest formats in many a day, with an unsightly painting on the dust-jacket and with a cover that resembles those volumes on Sane Sex Living by Dr. Long.)

Mr. DeJong, who has done far better things than what we have here, offers the farm family with much vague gloom, sentimentality, incongruous D. H. Lawrence touches, and dialogue of the sort that was so fulsomely admired in *Of Mice and Men*. There are two brothers, Ben and Joe, whom the author admires and evidently expects us to admire, steeped in the futility of an almost worthless farm. There are also an unadmirable father, a suffering mother, a grandfather who likes to steal the egg money (he dies), and the "dark sons," Bruce, Marius, and Sutton. Sutton does quite well in the illegal liquor game up to the time he is captured and put away. The lens that Mr. DeJong turns on these people is out of focus a good deal of the while, although I did enjoy a short section dealing with two of the brothers in Kansas City. On the other hand, you might not.

One does not think of Albert Halper as a particularly graceful writer, but certain enjoyable scenes in *Union Square*, and some of the stories in *On the Shore* seem masterly indeed compared with *Sons of the Fathers*. Here Mr. Halper always has his hand firmly on the most readily available stereotype, the awkward phrase, the unconvincing and hurried explanation. It is the story of Saul Bergman, a Jewish grocer who has left Russia for Chicago to escape service in the Czar's army. Saul goes from one grocery store to another in a series of failures, his family grows up, and militarism—this time the American variety—catches up with him again during the Wilsonian crusade. One of his sons attempts to elude the draft by homesteading; another is killed in France; and Saul Bergman's life is really over. The book is a plea for isolationism; and it is unfortunate, but only, I think, for Mr. Halper, that it is also a poor novel. The beating of drums by a new group of crusaders will limit its audience; but no more than the faults of the book itself.

To Be Continued

The problem of what to say about James Farrell at this stage of the game has given some of the critics a few, but only a few, uneasy moments. On the part of many of them it has become the custom, if not so far the requirement, in dealing with his later novels, to stretch out the phrase "More of the same," decry Mr. Farrell's geographical preoccupation and documentary fetish, and ask (hesitantly) the question, "How much longer is this to go on?" There is some justification for some parts of this method of treatment, for Mr. Farrell has covered more space in telling the story of the O'Neills and the O'Flahertys than he allowed himself for the whole of *Studs Lonigan*. The end still appears to be a long way off. Short of a mammoth catastrophe that would do away with all members of both families in a chapter or two—a most unlikely eventuality—it seems quite possible that the series which began with *A World I Never Made* is to be told in far more volumes than one would care to carry under one arm for any distance. Mr. Farrell, like M. Romains and M. Martin du Gard, is satisfied with nothing less than everything; and surely many readers, infirm or ailing or merely shaken momentarily by the insecurity and precariousness our civilization tenders us, must be asking themselves in the dead of the night: "Will I live to finish *Men of Good Will?* Will I still be here when Danny O'Neill matriculates at the University of Chicago?"

It is probably unnecessary by now to point out that Mr.

Review of *Father and Son* by James T. Farrell, *Partisan Review* 8 (May–June, 1941).

Farrell is long-winded, that he is stubborn, that he is often irritatingly repetitious; luckily for us, he is also one of the finest novelists of our time, and his faults are faults that he shares with some of the greatest writers. The task he has set for himself is staggering; that the task is carried out so thoroughly and so methodically continues to astonish us.

Father and Son brings us up to 1923 and is "more of the same" with a few notable differences. The bitter and the tender are both here, but it is the latter that is gaining ground. Priests and nuns, for instance, are no longer treated with the mailed fist Mr. Farrell used to employ on them; it is their individual differences that are stressed now. Lizz, Mrs. O'Flaherty, Peg, and Al—characters that were spotlighted previously—move into the background to make room for large performances by Jim O'Neill and his son, Danny. The novel is chiefly concerned with Jim's decline and end, and Danny's adolescence. Jim, after a lifetime of hard work, suffers a number of strokes and turns into a helpless paralytic, resigned and defeated. His death comes before there has been any real understanding between him and his son.

To his other accomplishments, Mr. Farrell has added that nearly impossible one—the creation of a believable and three-dimensional autobiographical hero. If there were symptoms, in the previous volumes, of a certain colorlessness in Danny O'Neill, they have vanished now. After such figures as Eugene Gant–George Webber—he of the goat-cry—we are relieved, but not surprised, to find that Mr. Farrell has given us something very remote from the usual "spokesman." His hero's jokes are bad, his taste worse; he is vain and his thoughts are ordinary, his opinions properly childish; the drunk he goes on is as honestly told as the exploits of Studs Lonigan. And yet Danny is highly sympathetic; the usual pat literary "sensitivity" has been scraped off to reveal the human. Danny O'Neill may be "against the world," but not in any romantic sense.

There is, I think, one most important reason for withholding certain judgments on the work on which Mr. Farrell is engaged at present. No one foresaw when reading the early volumes of the Lonigan trilogy—no one was capable of foreseeing—that the completed and collected work was to be far more powerful than even its three powerful sections. The bricks that Mr. Farrell laboriously assembled on his roof to topple over on the passerby were of an amazingly large number; but circumstances required that they be pushed off, originally, in three separate piles. This method stunned many; it was reasonably successful; but later, when they all went over at once—to drag out the metaphor to the bitter end—Mr. Farrell had succeeded in bringing off a vastly stronger and more lasting impact. What the O'Neill-O'Flaherty work will finally come to, with its wider canvas and its looser structure, it would be fantastic for anyone to predict. Mr. Farrell's effects are cumulative and not immediately apparent; in the mean time, while we wait, the individual volumes continue to be superbly readable.

The Poetry of Clark Mills

It is understandable enough that, during recent years, poets have been constantly beset by the temptation to take the state of the world as a more or less permanent subject. Only a small band has resisted such urges; a few have shut up talking and banged down the windows. No doubt a revolting little study might be made of the many poems produced during the past decade which take as their subject the world collapse—complex poems, but unmoving, most of them; the images as thick-coming and as artlessly arranged as the objects in a junk-pile, the music grunting and wheezing; a marked tendency toward metaphorical orgies; and always, of course, the note of prophetic tub-thumping, so popular this season. Certain poets, indeed, have even stumbled headlong toward what looks at first glance like an Eighth Type of Ambiguity; and bombast and subjectivity are fashionable again. What everyone feared has happened: poetry has become not less, but more "poetic."

This is not to say that admirable, and even excellent poems which scour the field have not recently appeared. They have; they have been scarce, however; and their authors have been men with something more than rococo vocabularies, uneasy consciences, and a way of charging in all directions at once. Mr. Mills (who was once apprenticed to the French Symbolists) would appear to be one of them.

In an early poem, "Catalina," published some years ago and, like many of his best poems, mysteriously omitted from both of these collections, Mr. Mills evinced a desire to "create

Review of *The Migrants* and *A Suite for France* by Clark Mills, *New Republic*, October 20, 1941.

some shadowy, figured myth." There could be no more apt description of what he has done in these books:

> The voices in our sleep called out, "Return."
> "Do not go north to meet the world." "Come back,
> patience is all." "O teach us to sit still."
> "Here is the limit you must never cross,
> the land you must not enter."
> The words whirled outward from the turning center
> of darkness; echoed among the caverns and the black
> passages of reflection, saying loss, and loss,
> whispering the immensity of time.
> We heard the words they spoke,
> like sound of water, climb;
> as one man's voice the multiple voices broke
> over the chill crest of Stalagmite Hill
> till we awoke.

For in "The Migrants"—a poem of some length in which the migration is emotional as well as geographical—we are sleepers awakening to find ourselves alone and afraid in an atmosphere of mist; simultaneously we stand high on a hill looking down upon the peopled landscape seeking "a way," and our seeking is a "long migration" which is ended only when "all at last may stand together." The legend appears again in other guises, notably in the epilogue, where again sleep is broken by "the shudder and the crash" of a familiar world, again fear presents itself, again the hilltop-seeking for "a way," and again the solution: "enter that new country."

It is scarcely a solution we have not heard before. And the myth is, it would seem, too shadowy, too vast. The effect, in spite of frequent references to such items as freight trains, headlines, loudspeakers, and iron birds on bomb routes, is essentially elusive and vague. Although the subject of the poem is the human situation, people in it are symbols seen only as abstractions, lying far away, like houses noted from an airplane. Too, Mr. Mills's lines, as mellifluous as one is likely to come upon in modern verse, are insufficiently relieved by the sharpness of which he is sometimes capable.

It is in the best lyrics of *A Suite for France* that the employment of fixed points of reference relaxes his dilemma of form. If the lines are as mellifluous as ever, the briefer form edges him to particulars which, though not minute, permit us glimpses of a sharper, less shadowy, landscape:

> And there below in the penumbra, the flamingos,
> tall on their pink stalks,
> inhabit bent perspectives; and in their cubicles
> the lemurs wait; and the gorillas nurse their stupor;
> and safe within rectangular horizons, the black panther
> pads without destination, or shores against the bars
> the deeper shadow of his vast despair.

His ear is very acute; his verse is always sensuous, adroit, and sustained. But what he hears is circumscribed; the sound of that smooth voice, like Mallarmé's or Swinburne's or Verlaine's, creates at times a desire for a rude interruption from a voice like John Skelton's or from Mr. Eliot as Krumpacker. Even so, Mr. Mills seems to me to be one of the few interesting poets under thirty. He is all in one piece, to begin with; and he would be interesting if only for the mannerisms he has resisted, while others flocked to them like dogs to a boneyard.

A Supplement from Cummings

There is little new one can say of Cummings. Arriving, as *50 Poems* does, shortly after his collected volume, it appears leaner than it actually is—merely addenda, a supplement one would have preferred bound with the key volume. And it would have been easy to predict, before its publication— more easily, perhaps, than with any other American poet— the almost exact ratio of good poems to bad that it would contain. From *Tulips and Chimneys* to *50 Poems,* the mean has been constant. If Mr. Cummings has at no time shown himself capable of separating the sheep from the goats, he has at least done something better: he has not yet given us a book that revealed an alarming switch or falling off.

Indeed, the preservation of the Cummings personality, which has been recently diagnosed elsewhere in terms of utmost denigration, would seem to be something of a minor miracle in an age specializing in insecurity, violent change, and shifts of opinion equally violent. If the cost of this conservation on Mr. Cummings's part has been a lack of "progression"—and, I suppose, it has been; if the ravages of his anti-intellectualism are everywhere to be seen—and they are; and if even the most delightful personalities can have us yawning some midnights, there has been the not inconsiderable compensation that Mr. Cummings's lapses have been constant throughout his career. That set of attitudes which he has

Review of *50 Poems* by E. E. Cummings, *Poetry,* December, 1941. Copyright 1941 by The Modern Poetry Association. Reprinted by permission of the Editor of *Poetry.*

developed and preserved through nearly twenty-five years of writing add up to what one might regard as one of the few "personalities" completely expressed in American poetry. With the usual exceptions, what we have had largely in other quarters has been a succession of masks, somewhat awry.

This personality has carried along with it, unhappily, such embarrassments as the frequently unsuccessful typographical tricks; the "little silent Christmas tree," "the wisti-twisti barberpole," and the "queer old balloon man," all of which could enter one of Ralph Hodgson's poems (or one of Christopher Morley's essays) with no trouble at all; and an inverted sentimentality that is only a little more forgivable. At his best, however—and he is at his best some of the time in all his books—there are only a handful of living poets to rank with him. One might profitably select from his lyrics, his satires, his ballads, and his experiments a collection to stand with almost any of his contemporaries. And some of the poems from this book would be in it:

> anyone lived in a pretty how town
> (with up so floating many bells down)
> spring summer autumn winter
> he sang his didn't he danced his did.
>
> Women and men (both little and small)
> cared for anyone not at all
> they sowed their isn't they reaped their same
> sun moon stars rain

$$*\qquad*\qquad*$$

> my father moved through dooms of love
> through sames of am through haves of give
> singing each morning out of each night
> my father moved through depths of height

$$*\qquad*\qquad*$$

> moon
> 's whis-
> per
> in sunset

or thrushes toward dusk among whippoorwills or
tree field rock hollyhock forest brook chickadee
mountain. Mountain)
whycoloured worlds of because do

not stand against yet which is built by
forever & sunsmell
(sometimes a wonder
of wild roses

sometimes)
with north
over
the barn

Sixteen Hundred Poems

Mr. Aldington's *Viking Book of Poetry* is physically, if not other-
wise, heavy. Reprinting nearly thirteen hundred poems by
some three hundred poets, it is 1,272 pages long, contains
good indexes and bibliographies, is a distinguished piece of
bookmaking, and takes one from Beowulf to Delmore
Schwartz. Mr. Aldington refers to it as a "general" rather than
"personal" anthology, and "popular and aesthetic" rather than
"academic and historical." In his introduction, masked as a
chatty letter to his publisher, Mr. Aldington puts his cards on
the table. He has reread the complete works of the poets
quoted and built his book around a "self-selecting nucleus of
universally admired poems"; he has not been able to put in
everything he wanted, but what is left out seems to him "com-
paratively unimportant"; he has taken into account, in the
choice of his selections, "certain human limitations." Poets of
the Tudor-Stuart period and the nineteenth century win his
especial praise. Browning, he thinks, was the last "really ma-
jor" poet produced by England. Recent and contemporary
poets, if they get in at all, are represented on a token basis.
Parody and nonsense verses are under no circumstances to
show themselves here; they are "outside the book's logical
scheme." "Though usually light-hearted," says Mr. Aldington
warningly, "parody can sometimes be cruel."

Review of *The Viking Book of Poetry of the English-Speaking World*
edited by Richard Aldington and *Reading Poems: An Introduction to
Critical Study* edited by Wright Thomas and Stuart Gerry Brown,
Poetry, March, 1942. Copyright 1942 by The Modern Poetry Associa-
tion. Reprinted by permission of the Editor of *Poetry*.

The selections are largely disappointing. One is pleased to find, among others, the poem by Chidiock Tichbourne, two by T. E. Hulme, and Smart's *Song to David,* but except in cases where choice reduces itself to one or two categorical imperatives, Mr. Aldington shows a well-developed knack for missing the point. (See, as examples, his work on Emily Dickinson, Hardy, and Beddoes.) The angry, the intensely religious, the political, and the obscure sides of many poets are kept carefully under cover, and in spite of the editor's avowed intention to "eliminate the sentimental," a noticeably bulky residue remains. Mr. Aldington is out for few revaluations: Bobbie Burns, for instance, gets more space than Hardy, Donne, and Emily Dickinson put together. Among the omissions: Crabbe, Traherne, Vachel Lindsay, William Chamberlayne, Cleland, Edward De Vere, Addison, Watts, and Trumbull Stickney; Lear and Lewis Carroll are of course barred because they wrote "nonsense verses." On the other hand, few anthologies have included so many poems in praise of womankind; they give the book whatever *geist* it may have. There are no hymns, no limericks, no American ballads (though early English ballads are well represented).

We have long awaited an Englishman with a knowledge, an understanding, and an appreciation of American poetry; the search goes on; Mr. Aldington is clearly not our man. One can see how a more blurred selection from contemporary American verse might have been made, but not easily. Rather typical is his reprinting of William Carlos Williams's *Peace on Earth,* a very early lyric thoroughly unrepresentative of either the body of Williams's work or of his best work. It is as though an editor of a volume of American prose represented Hemingway solely by his contribution to the June 1917 number of *Senior Tabula,* yearbook of the Oak Park (Ill.) High School. And when that tireless informant, the flap on the dust jacket, points out that satirical verse is "liberally represented," one turns to find what satirical poems of Lawrence, Pound, Eliot, and Cummings are included. The thought occurs that perhaps the Hippopotamus, Mauberly, and the Cambridge ladies may appear. They do not; nor do others similar to these poems; we are given only the "other side" of these men.

They, too, I suppose, can "sometimes be cruel." Among the living, Mr. Aldington finds room for Ralph Chaplin, Joseph Campbell, Edward Davison, Eric Robertson Dobbs, Leonard Bacon, and Anna Wickham; but none for John Peale Bishop, Louise Bogan, Horace Gregory—many interesting lists might be drawn up. Osbert Sitwell gets more space than Ezra Pound. It would seem that the editor's admiration for the nineteenth century has resulted in an anthology in which the viewpoint of that century shows on many more pages than the ones directly given over to it.

Thomas and Brown's *Reading Poems* is a compilation for the classroom, designed chiefly for those "who may wish to emphasize the skills of reading rather than the history of poetry." The shadow of Mr. I. A. Richards falls quietly over the volume: the selections—which are excellent, and which begin with simple lyrics and progress to *The Waste Land*—are printed without benefit of the authors' names, though these appear elsewhere in an appendix with notes. Some three hundred poems are included, as well as reproductions of successive drafts of poems by Tennyson, Keats, Spender, and Auden. Even with its atmosphere of chalk-dust and corridor, this is a valuable anthology.

Parts

But a World

Wallace Stevens has been, and still is, very much what Van Wyck Brooks has blithely called a "coterie writer." His audience is probably more restricted than that of any other poet of his importance. A good many of the poets of Mr. Stevens's generation, and of the generation following, have, in their various ways—some after prolonged experimental maneuvers—entered doors of political discipleship, stale recapitulation, critical inflexibility, or silence. Stevens has been one of the few to have escaped all of these easily available traps; and he has been publishing for more than forty years. Since 1899, the year in which his first uncertain verses appeared in the *Harvard Advocate,* he has irregularly but persistently continued to document the exploration of his fanciful, bizarre, and original world, parts of which are on exhibition here.

Self-conscious, ironic, impersonal, Stevens produced in *Harmonium,* his first book, the most exhaustive poetic record we have had of the interrelationships of the world of fact and the artistic imagination. Almost every poem he has written has been an exercise in ransacking the shifting antagonisms of opposites, employing an imagery more varied and luxuriant than any other of the time. Opulent cataracts, apricots, pale parasols, bougainvilleas, peacocks, and purple watermelons swarmed through his early poems; the "literary" and the commonplace were juxtaposed in patterns of the most striking and lustrous variety. No other poet has displayed a

Review of *Parts of a World* by Wallace Stevens, *New Republic,* September 28, 1942.

greater facility for inventing diversified symbols for relatively similar purposes.

The world of this volume, extending and deepening the concern with society toward which Stevens has been moving ever since the publication of *Ideas of Order* seven years ago, bears a closer relationship to the objective world of today than that earlier world of *Harmonium*—civilized, elegant, and lush—had to the Wilson-Harding-Coolidge world of its composition. Here one finds less of the Firbankian vaudeville, the dazzle, the oo-la-la, that skittered among the poet's earlier balancings between the luxuriant and the austere.

In the face of today's disintegration and chaos, a good deal of his earlier serenity and self-possession has gone. There are new tones of anguish, grief, and disgust, and an awareness that our society is moving not to "the bread and wine of the mind," but to "a falling and an end." The accessibility of the imagination as a place of retreat has been blocked more and more by "the bombastic intimations of winter," "the martyrs à la mode," the "soldiers . . . marching and marching in a tragic time":

> It is shaken now. It will burst into flames,
> Either now or tomorrow or the day after that.

Stevens was never blind to threatenings of disaster; but his awareness of it, and the manner in which it was faced, were rendered a bit remote by a general air of languid fastidiousness—disaster faced in the drawing-room with a glass of sherry and a collection of Picassos. Now his speculations on a society in which the imagination may very well be liquidated conclude with the melancholy reflection that

> In a village of the indigenes,
> One would have still to discover. Among the dogs and dung
> One would continue to contend with one's ideas.

An increasing despair runs through these poems, and it is most marked in some of the finest lyrics, in "The Dwarf," "Loneliness in New Jersey," "Dry Loaf," "Arcades of Philadelphia the Past," in which mountains, at first recalled with nostalgia, become "scratched and used, pure fakes"; "The Common Life," in which the bleakness of the objective world is scrutinized as a dimensionless horror; and in "Cuisine Bourgeoise," in which

> We feast on human heads, brought in on leaves,
> Crowned with the first, cold buds. On these we live,
> No longer on the ancient cake of seed,
> The almond and deep fruit. This bitter meat
> Sustains us. . . . Who, then, are they, seated here?
> Is the table a mirror in which they sit and look?
> Are they men eating reflections of themselves?

Stevens has never specialized in intensity; the absence of it, in many of the other poems, combined with a growing rhetorical monotony, accounts for most of his failures. There are mobs and masses in his poetry that were never here before; and there is even one fairly long poem that gives evidence of being the outcome of a brief tête-à-tête with Marxism. And there are a few poems looking like ill-at-ease revivals of standard Stevens favorites, but they are not frequent. His distinguished place in American poetry has never been more secure.

A note on format: Some person—a Knopf employee or perhaps the author—has seen fit to leave a disturbingly large amount of white space between sentence-breaks, and, in some cases, after commas, but without uniformity. Typographically, it is a most unpleasant device; and it makes many of the poems look as though they were falling apart on the page, or in need of a little glue.

Miss Rukeyser's Marine Poem

There's one thing you can say about Muriel: she's not lazy.

Review of *Wake Island* by Muriel Rukeyser, *Partisan Review* 9 (November–December, 1942). Reprinted by permission.

John Cheever's Stories

In 1930, when he was seventeen, John Cheever severed his connections with an Eastern preparatory school, and not long afterwards appeared in this magazine with a sensitive and precocious account of the institution in which he had been a most unhappy student. It was a very promising piece of work. Cheever went on to publish stories at infrequent intervals in the little magazines of the early 1930s; but it was not until the *New Yorker*, shrewdly detecting a writer of talent, took him up only a few years ago that he suddenly displayed an unexpected knack for rapidly turning out neatly tailored sketches for that magazine, most of them acid accounts of pathos in the suburbs.

As examples of fiction from the *New Yorker,* these stories of Mr. Cheever's are among the best that have appeared there recently, and this is particularly true of those which exploit a cool and narrow-eyed treatment of tensions arising from the war. Mr. Cheever's drunken draft-dodger and his young draftee are particularly well managed, and the sketches in which they appear are quite unblemished by the pieties and embarrassments which ordinarily mark war fiction published while a war is on. Many of the other stories—and if my count is right, all but six of the thirty included here are from the *New Yorker*—have not improved by their being collected in a book. As individual magazine stories they seemed better than they are; read one after another, their nearly identical lengths, similarities of tone and situation, and their somehow remote

Review of *The Way Some People Live* by John Cheever, *New Republic,* April 19, 1943.

and unambitious style, produce an effect of sameness and eventually of tedium. The formula has been flourished too obviously and too often.

Mr. Cheever is not alone. He bathes in that same large municipal pool where all *New Yorker* short-story writers swim and sink. As Lionel Trilling remarked, one feels that almost any one of them might write another's story. Their characters live in an identical and tidy world which the magazine's editors have laboriously created by a set tone and by an elaborate hierarchy of taboos. It is a milieu which the writers stray from only at their peril. From Mr. Cheever's bleak suburban homes to Sally Benson's nurseries, or to John O'Hara's night clubs (Chicago, Hollywood, and New York), or to Edward Newhouse's bars, it is only a step. The reader need scarcely move. Few magazines of the time have had so bright and professional an air, and fewer others have attained so high a level of general skill in their prose. But it is skill expended on what is more often than not the essentially trivial; it would even seem that the magazine's character demands a patina of triviality spread over those themes and situations which its policy allows. Its writers must frequently entertain themselves by concentrating on the merely decorative qualities of a scene, a restriction brought on by an understandable hesitancy to explore their material deeply. Thus, in such a story as Mr. Cheever's "Forever Hold Your Peace," the exhaustively reported small talk of guests at a wedding performs the services of a more consequential and telling method of viewing the situation.

Some of Mr. Cheever's best stories, which were written during his less fettered pre–*New Yorker* phase—particularly "The Teaser" and "The Princess," which came out in this magazine some years ago, and "Behold a Cloud in the West," from *New Letters*—have been mysteriously omitted. So have a number of others that would stand up better than many that are here. But one long story, "Of Love: A Testimony," which is seven or eight years old, has been retained. It is an excellent example of what this writer is capable of doing when he is his own man, when he has room enough in which to work for something more than episodic notation and minor perceptive effects.

II

The Partisan at *Time*, 1943–49

The New Pictures

The Phantom of the Opera (Universal) contains more opera than phantom, more trills than thrills. In this it differs from the original *Phantom,* which Universal produced in the shock-absorbing twenties as a shivery vehicle for the late multiform Lon Chaney. The 1943 Phantom is bantam-sized Claude Rains, who attempts to terrify by sheer force of character, scar tissue, and Technicolor. Scuttling about in a robin's-egg blue mask, Cinemactor Rains scares nobody but his fellow cinemactors.

A sensitive bit of casting finally lands Baritone Nelson Eddy in his first horror picture. Here Eddy is Anatole Carron of the Paris Opera, who loves operatic Understudy Christine Dubois (Susanna Foster). She seems fated to go on understudying indefinitely until befriended by Enrique Claudin (Claude Rains). For Christine, Claudin has a vast but secret passion. [When he is] fired from the orchestra, a pan of acid is thrown at him, [which] starts him on his exhilarating career as [the] Phantom.

To further Christine's career he steals the master key of the opera house, puts a Mickey Finn into Christine's rival's drink, sends poison-pen letters, strangles a soprano and her maid, saws a huge chandelier from its chain during the performance of an opera in which Christine's rival is singing. The hard-pressed Sûreté (French FBI) ultimately has to call on Composer Franz Liszt (German Shakesperian Actor Fritz Leiber) to aid them in bagging the cagey Phantom.

Time, August 23 and 30, 1943. Copyright 1943 Time Inc. All rights reserved. Reprinted by permission from *Time.*

Above Suspicion (MGM) is something new in Joan Crawford pictures. Instead of setting a special table for her saucer-eyed talents, it all but relegates Miss Crawford to playing stooge to pouty Fred MacMurray. Still worse, Joan's usually endless array of hats is reduced to a bare subsistence level.

MacMurray and Crawford are an American and his bride in prewar Germany, but not on anything so innocent as a honeymoon. In quest of a secret which Great Britain needs to know they get involved in disguises, a Liszt-accompanied murder, battles with the Gestapo. They also run afoul of such suspicious figures as Basil Rathbone and Conrad Veidt. Strangely enough, it all adds up to a better-than-average summertime melodrama.

But for Miss Crawford it is not much of an event to mark her departure from MGM, where she has been a big name ever since the gin-drenched days of *Our Dancing Daughters* (1928). Her new boss: Warner's. Reported inducement: "an executive job."

For Conrad Veidt *Above Suspicion* is also a milestone: his last picture for anybody. He died last spring, age fifty, of a heart attack, on a Hollywood golf course. Often regarded as Eric von Stroheim's most formidable rival as a fondler of monocles, German-born Veidt first came to fame in Robert Wiene's bizarre fantasy, *The Cabinet of Dr. Caligari.* Other weirdies, like *The Hands of Mr. Orlac,* followed. Women fainted, men screamed, children chortled when they were shown. By 1926, when Veidt went to Hollywood, audiences had got hold of themselves pretty well, but his adroit villainy was always good for a hiss.

How Tom Is Doin'

Radio listeners who tuned in the Blue Network's Chamber Music Society of Lower Basin Street last Sunday night heard a mammoth left hand beating out the solidest bass in U.S. pianism, a right hand doing fine and jubilant things. The hands were those of the great Thomas Wright ("Fats") Waller, short-time student of Leopold Godowsky and lifelong admirer of James P. Johnson, the great professor of Jamaica, Long Island. Even a tyro in such matters might easily guess what experts have known for years: that Fats Waller is the pay-off in the classic American jazz piano style—full-chorded and hallelujah.

Of late the Waller hands have not been idle. In the motion picture *Stormy Weather,* they caused a battered piano to romp in rare fashion. For the Broadway musical *Early to Bed,* the Waller right hand picked out the tunes. This week, back in Manhattan after a trip to Canada, Fats Waller was cooking up some new numbers.

He has cooked up some good ones before. Among them: "Ain't Misbehavin'," "I've Got a Feelin' I'm Fallin'," "Keepin' Out of Mischief Now." Waller has collaborated with many a lyricist. Some of his best results he turned out with Andy Razaf,* his favorite poet next to Longfellow. During one rewarding session in retreat at Asbury Park, New Jersey, the two men turned out "Zonky," "My Fate Is in Your Hands,"

Time, August 9, 1943. Copyright 1943 Time Inc. All rights reserved. Reprinted by permission from *Time.*

*Razaf's real name: Andrea Razafinkeriefo. He is the nephew of Ranavalona III, last queen of Madagascar.

and "Honeysuckle Rose" in two hours. Razaf had enticed Waller into his mother's Asbury Park home for a productive session away from the nightspots. Says Razaf: "She's a wonderful cook and Fats loves to eat. We had a show to write and I figured that would keep Fats away from the bars. He could set the telephone book to music."

Keeping Tom Waller away from bars is a difficult feat. His capacity for both food and drink is vast. A Waller breakfast may include six pork chops. It is when he is seated at the piano that he most relishes a steady supply of gin. When his right-hand man, brother-in-law Louis Rutherford, enters with a tray of glasses, Tom will cry, "Ah, here's the man with the dream wagon! I want it to hit me around my edges and get to every pound."

The Early Days

That requires a lot of alcohol: Waller is five feet ten and weighs over 270 pounds. That mass helps to account for the great strength of his basses, and makes his playing look as magisterial as it sounds. Whether he plays a stomping "Dinah" or lazy variations on "When My Baby Smiles at Me," no other pianist gives quite his impression of commanding ease. Musicians he plays with sense it instantly, ease up themselves.

Fats was playing a harmonium at the age of five. Born on Manhattan's West One Hundred and Thirty-fourth Street, he grew up next door to P.S. 89. This made it easy for his mother, who had eleven other children, to lean out of the window and call, "How's Tom doin'?" His father was pastor of the Abyssinian Baptist Church, now the largest Baptist congregation in the world, where Tom took up the organ.

At fourteen, Tom had a steady job on the organ in Harlem's Lincoln Theater. He made Q.R.S. piano rolls, records with blues-singers Bessie Smith and Sarah Martin. The late Arnold Rothstein backed Waller's first show, *Keep Shufflin'*. On records, Waller began to sing as well as play, and in his expressive mouth the inane words of a popular song often came in for very searching satirical treatment. In 1929, in collaboration with guitarist Eddie Condon and a small but vital ensemble, he made one of the greatest jazz records of all time: "The Minor Drag" and "Harlem Fuss."

The Paris Period

In 1932 Fats balked the depression with a rapid month in Paris. There his enthusiastic friends included Marcel Dupré, one-time organist of Notre Dame Cathedral. With Dupré, Fats climbed into the Notre Dame organ loft where "first he played on the god box, then I played on the god box." In Paris Fats also came into cultural contact with a fellow pianist and ex-patriate named "Steeplehead" Johnson. Fats got home from the French capital by wiring Irving Berlin for funds.

Few who had funds could ever refuse him. With a piano, a bottle of gin, and a hot weather handkerchief, he is one of the most infectious men alive. With his wife Anita and their two musically gifted sons, Maurice, fifteen, and Ronald, fourteen, he lives in an eight-room English brick house in St. Albans, Long Island. The house has a Hammond organ, a size B Steinway grand, and an automatic phonograph with fifteen hundred records. Next to Lincoln and FDR, Fats considered Johann Sebastian Bach the greatest man in history.

Once a dewy-eyed young thing stopped Fats and inquired, "Mr. Waller, what is swing?" Said he: "Lady, if you got to ask, you ain't got it."

No Thanks

Although the field of hot music has proved a fruitful one for some of its historians and critics, the novelists of jazz have generally approached this calling with all the heavy-handedness of the zealot. Qualities of frenzy and belief control them; except for Dorothy Baker's *Young Man with a Horn,* which touched off the trend, not one of the novels of jazz musicians' lives has approximated even the satisfactions of a second-rate jam session.

Mr. George Willis's *Tangleweed,* the most recent product of this school, is stuck fast in the same groove. His brief and haphazard collection of sketches, fitfully masquerading as a novel, deals with the lives of a drummer, a pianist, and a trumpet man who play in a small Kansas City jazz band. Most of Mr. Willis's space is devoted to a love story of the sort the Macfadden publications handle more skillfully, and to lengthy rhapsodic passages dealing with such matters as the exhilaration of musical performance, anxiety, the Earth, America. Mr. Willis describing a cow is something not to miss. "Her massive body," he writes, "was well hung between the wide, solid shoulders, and her large udder was easily available."

The influence of Thomas Wolfe on Mr. Willis has been considerable; his hep-cats can emit tortured goat-cries with the most agonized members of the Gant family. Miss Ann Chidester's submission to the Wolfesque manner is so complete that her writing takes on interest only as an example of

---

Review of *Tangleweed* by George Willis; *No Longer Fugitive* by Ann Chidester; *Daylight on Saturday* by J. B. Priestley; and *Survival* by Phyllis Bottome, *New Republic,* October 11, 1943.

imitation. Miss Chidester's Liam Moore, age twenty, is a Young Man in Search of Himself. Liam is pretty much of a cynic, given to saying "Bilge!" with some heat to those who disagree with him about the war. Liam appears to be on the edge of declaring himself a conscientious objector. Never will he fight, etc. But by page 286, after much soul-searching in St. Paul, Bismarck, and points south, he finds that his whole desire is "to shape with others the golden days of tomorrow." This is Miss Chidester's way of saying that her hero is itching to enlist.

Golden-day-shaping Liam works intermittently as a swing clarinetist, and this gives Miss Chidester a chance to work the magic of her rhetoric on music. The following passage supposedly describes a hot clarinet solo by Pee Wee Russell, one of the musicians mentioned in the book whose name is spelled correctly:

> The music began slow, easy as the rising of a bird over a prairie land with spaces of sky to twirl in and to fall. It began like the timid prayer of a child, sank into fallow fields, drew forth the lovely water-crested sprouts, shot up, fell down, wept and bespoke a heart of darkness. It went on in a torrent like an ageless river, like a woman in red slippers tottering slightly. . . .

Mr. Willis and Miss Chidester are inspired though quite untalented amateurs. Mr. J. B. Priestley and Miss Phyllis Bottome are professionals to the marrow, each with a long-seasoned familiarity with the craft that produces Literary Guild novels and serials in the more forward-looking women's magazines. The embarrassing egomaniacal yearnings of the Wolfe-pack are not for them: their first novels, indeed, had the settled and solid air of the prematurely middle-aged. Surely at no time were they ever Lost at all. Here are objectivity, topicality, the Popular; these writers are centrists in the long rank and file of British hackdom.

Daylight on Saturday, Mr. Priestley's fortieth book, is an English wartime version of that worrisome and once hotly debated Bolshevist article, the Collective Novel. Mr. Priestley races hurriedly through the main factory of the Elmdown Aircraft Co., Ltd.—it has "beastly machines" that scream "like great wounded animals"—and brings in a number of rather breathless reports on its workers. His findings include many old Dickens-Priestley types, good companions unchanged, most of them, by the war. It is a readable, metallic, and rather unreal book.

Miss Phyllis Bottome first published her psychological novel, *Survival,* in the pages of the *Ladies' Home Journal. Survival* is a not untypical example of women's magazine fiction—Mrs. Humphrey Ward might have written thus of psychoanalysis. ("'And you think *love* is War to the Knife?' he asked me incredulously, his dark thin eyebrows rising, without insolence this time, in a sort of pained wonder.") A Jewish refugee doctor, a disciple of Adler (Miss Bottome is a confirmed Adlerian), escapes from Vienna to England in the spring of 1939. With a backdrop of bombs falling on Plymouth, Dr. von Rittenhaus turns a country estate into a hospital and investigates upper-crust neuroses.

These four novels, brought out by four different publishers in the same month, are fairly typical of the present output. They are serious, but only in their intentions. Not one of them has the entertainment value of the average detective story, nor can they be said to be as well written; their characters are sticks; their authors are, in these books at least, incapable of writing half a page without employing the dreariest clichés. It would seem that the paper shortage we hear so much about is less worrisome than we have been led to believe.

Musicians' Potpourri

Mr. Siegmeister is a young and prolific musical popularizer whose own writings reveal him as one of music's busiest and most enthusiastic press agents. "With the growth of radio, good music . . . has won its way into the hearts of Americans everywhere," he writes, pulling out the *vox humana* and xylophone stops. "When Beethoven is heard in hot-dog stands, César Franck in filling stations between changes of oil, and Stravinsky played in every fifteen-cent movie house throughout the country (what matter if it be through the medium of Disney's grinning dinosaurs?) it is clear that the old bars are down."

They are indeed, and in his anthology Mr. Siegmeister makes no attempt to put them back up. *The Music Lover's Handbook* is less a handbook or cyclopedia than a sort of overstuffed grab-bag of extracts from books, articles, and notes by over fifty "outstanding musical figures."

Here are essays on the techniques of composition, on musical forms, opera, the ballet (an excellent one by Lincoln Kirstein), over forty articles on composers from Palestrina to Morton Gould, reminiscences of the editor's boyhood, and some sixty program notes. Such assorted pieces as "Why Not Try the Air?" by Davidson Taylor, "Listening to Modern Music," by Deems Taylor, and "Concert Music in Barnum's Day," by David Ewen, rattle noisily against each other. Stravinsky

Review of *The Music Lover's Handbook* edited by Elie Siegmeister, *New York Times Book Review,* October 17, 1943. Copyright © 1943 by The New York Times Company. Reprinted by permission.

reports how he wrote "Petroushka," Shostakovich's wife is interviewed, Benny Goodman describes his early days, Winthrop Sargeant discusses jazz with an astringency and clarity which that division of music seldom receives. There is considerable material on the musical contribution of Negroes; and a valuable and well-edited section devoted to folk music, which is very possibly the book's real "contribution." Thomas Jefferson is a strange name to come upon. He writes on "Planning an Orchestra." Benjamin Franklin offers "On Setting Words to Music." Something is here, as they say, for everybody.

No less than twenty-three of the articles are by Mr. Siegmeister himself. Some readers, oversensitive to the presence in his work of such exclamatory nifties as "Dangerous thoughts!" and "Fateful gesture!" may find twenty-three too many. They may also be taken aback by his excursions into autobiography, his exaltation of "down-to-earth" qualities, and his hail-fellow-traveler-well-met resourcefulness which enables him to salute Mozart as "a poet of democracy coming to birth."

Mr. Siegmeister has obviously searched hard for material that is popular, anecdotal, informative, and "readable." He has found a considerable amount. But when he writes that "another editor might prepare a volume with quite different contents," one can only agree most heartily. Since this is, in the editor's words, a very large book designed to include "many sorts of writing—scholarly, gay, intimate, casual, passionate," quite a few writers come to mind who were not invited to attend Mr. Siegmeister's free-for-all. There is nothing by Tovey, Einstein, Paul Rosenfeld, Huneker, Eric Blom, Gerald Abraham, or W. J. Turner. (Turner on Mozart and Abraham on Mussorgsky would have been something of an improvement on Mr. Siegmeister, who handles both composers for the volume.) Paul Henry Lang, B. H. Haggin, and J. W. N. Sullivan are others among the missing.

Champion of Failures

"There is a photograph of Bourne as a child of about seven," writes Louis Filler, "his hair carefully combed over his left ear to hide a deformity. And in a picture of his high school graduation class he stands, more than a head shorter than the girls, back in the last row, obviously placed to hide as much as possible of his dwarfed body."

This boy, a stunted hunchback with a twisted face, was to become one of the most unusual and gifted writers of his time, and a courageous and heroic spokesman for a part of his generation. His close friend, Van Wyck Brooks, was to write that "no other young American critic . . . exhibited so clear a tendency, so coherent a body of desires. His personality was not only unique, it was also absolutely expressive. . . . I have had the delightful experience of reading through at a sitting, so to say, the whole mass of his uncollected writings, articles, essays, book reviews, unprinted fragments, and a few letters, and I am astonished at the way in which, like a ball of camphor in a trunk, the pungent savor of the man spreads itself over every paragraph. . . . Here was Emerson's American Scholar at last, but radiating an infinitely warmer, profaner, more companionable influence than Emerson had ever dreamed of, an influence that savored rather of Whitman and William James." After Bourne's death twenty-five years had to pass before a biography of him—this volume by Mr. Filler—was published.

Review of *Randolph Bourne* by Louis Filler, *New York Times Book Review*, October 31, 1943. Copyright © 1943 by The New York Times Company. Reprinted by permission.

Randolph Silliman Bourne was born in Bloomfield, New Jersey, in 1886. His deformity was of a nature scarcely calculated to make his childhood a happy one, and he soon turned to music as an escape from the sense of alienation, subdued or intense, he was always to feel. What Bourne wanted most was friendship, inadequately provided by Bloomfield; and the lack of it was to intensify his sympathy for losers, rebels, and outcasts.

"It makes me wince," Bourne wrote later, "to hear a man spoken of as a failure, or to have it said of one that he 'doesn't amount to much.' Instantly I want to know why he has not succeeded, and what have been the forces that have been working against him. He is the truly interesting person, and yet how little our eager-pressing, on-rushing world cares about such aspects of life, and how hideously though unconsciously cruel and heartless it usually is!"

Not until six years after graduation from high school was Bourne able to enter college. During that dismal interlude he spent most of his time cutting player-piano rolls at five cents a foot. When his rate was reduced to four and a half cents he moved to New York. In 1909, after several years of stagnation, he was offered a scholarship at Columbia University.

By that time Bourne had become a Socialist. His conversion had flowered, his biographer writes, through "a conversation with a legless cripple who wheeled himself about in a chair. Their discussion took place in the basement of the New York Public Library, where the cripple became so excited and talked so loudly that they were both asked to leave the building."

Columbia gave Bourne the response he needed. Frederick Keppel, later to become the guiding hand of the Carnegie Corporation and then dean of the college, was of great help to him; and at Columbia Bourne first met Carl Zigrosser, Charles Beard, Carl Van Doren, John Dewey. He received many prizes and fellowships, became a regular contributor to the *Atlantic Monthly,* and while still at the university published a volume of his essays.

A Gilder Fellowship made it possible for Bourne to travel in Europe. Of the people he saw and met, Chesterton struck him as "gluttonous and thick, with something tricky and unsavory about him." Sidney Webb seemed to have "the patient air of a man expounding arithmetic to backward children." Of the English middle-class reformers, only Shaw seemed admirable.

England, on the whole, depressed Bourne; France was far more to his liking. There he made many friends, among them Jules Romains. In Germany he was repelled by "something in the soul of the people which I cannot make articulate . . . a sort of thickness and sentimentality and a lack of critical sense. . . ." It was August, 1914, "The wheels of the clock," Bourne wrote, "have completely stopped in Europe."

He came back to an America bustling with Socialist and literary movements, convinced that it could stay out the war. Bourne was picked up by Herbert Croly to write for the magazine he was launching, the *New Republic.* That magazine was pleased to print Bourne's work so long as it devoted its attention to such topics as town planning, progressive education, and the Gary schools—about which Bourne wrote a book and helped bring nationwide attention to the theories of John Dewey.

The *New Republic*'s interest in free speech was not, however, extensive enough to make room for Bourne's increasingly acid comments on the behavior of intellectuals in wartime, his attacks on Dewey's pragmatism, his unwavering pacifism.

"In a time of faith," he wrote, "skepticism is the most intolerable of insults." The *New Republic* dispensed with Bourne's services. The *Seven Arts,* another magazine to which he contributed some of his best work, had its subsidy withdrawn. "War," Bourne wrote during this period, "is the health of the State."

Magazines would have none of this. He could no longer publish his articles. He gave up his apartment and took a small furnished room, where he turned more and more to literature, music, and conversation. Three days before Christmas, in 1918, he died of bronchial pneumonia in a cheap Greenwich Village rooming-house.

Coates's Short Stories

It is difficult, in reviewing a book of short stories reprinted from the *New Yorker,* to separate the writer from the magazine. Probably no other publication adheres to so carefully set a tone in its fiction. Its somewhat unadventurous rhetoric, its insularity, its limited geography of situation, its careful manipulations of pathos—all these, to some extent, are shared by those who write its short stories.

Mr. Coates's pieces—all but six originally appeared in the *New Yorker*—exhibit, not unnaturally, all these characteristics. The collection offers, in addition, a good illustration of Mr. Coates's dual-purpose ego. His non–*New Yorker* work has frequently been of a Dadaist or Expressionist nature; but this "real" personality—the one responsible for his bizarre and satirical detective story, "The Eater of Darkness," and his experimental novel of Manhattan life, *Yesterday's Burdens*—is not to be found here. Although the stories in *All the Year Round* are skillful and rather typical examples of the *New Yorker*'s fiction, there is more variety to be found in it than in most of such one-man shows. Part of this can be accounted for by Coates's interest in a wider range of characters and by the inclusion of stories which build toward considerable intensity through their employment of violent patterns of action.

Too often, however, the upsets and disorders toward which his stories frequently build seem contrived. In "Begin-

---

Review of *All the Year Round* by Robert M. Coates, *New York Times Book Review,* December 12, 1943. Copyright © 1943 by The New York Times Company. Reprinted by permission.

ning of a Journey," a boy meets his sister on a street corner and announces that he is going to run away from home. Her refusal to lend him twenty dollars and his suspicions of her own corruption prompt him to shove her into a vestibule and hit her in the face with his fist. The objectivity of Coates's method here, which serves his purposes better in certain other stories, acts as a sort of blackout in which motivations are difficult to glimpse.

There are a number of stories that take place in Manhattan bars and on its streets—brief snapshots of the frustrated and irritable; and a greater number of stories which deal with farm life. Those in the first division are sharp, bitter, and often very effectively written; Coates's investigations of the bucolic are inclined to be a bit tepid and protracted.

It is in such pieces as "The Fury" and "One Night at Coney," both of which deal with sexually abnormal individuals faced with mob violence, and in "The Darkness of the Night," which concerns itself with the events leading up to a murder, that Coates is seen to best advantage. These are three very good stories indeed. They succeed in taking their distance from the majority of his stories by becoming sharp communications of terror rather than quick takes of a situation or mere exercises in suspense.

"Over Six Hundred Cartoons . . ."

The insistent tastelessness with which Mr. Craven has con-
verted the Benton-Curry-Wood school of painting into an
American Renaissance is now dragged into service as a tool to
help in the assembling of "the best American humorous car-
toons from the turn of the Century to the present." A natural
for Simon and Schuster at a time when collections of cartoons
are selling in phenomenally large editions (from Thurber,
Whitney Darrow, and Addams on down to *Esquire* contrib-
utors and Private Breger), Mr. Craven's book is the most am-
bitious attempt yet to survey this field of popular art.

Over six hundred cartoons from 1883 to 1943 are in-
cluded. These have been slapped into place in a maddening
chronological order that could not be bettered for promoting
a lack of understanding of the cartoon's development in this
country. Anything, indeed, goes: political cartoons, comic
strips, and the "social cartoon" are jumbled together with
nothing but dates of publication to link them. After reprint-
ing a number of early political cartoons, Mr. Craven dis-
penses with later examples on the grounds that they fail to
amuse him. (His criteria of selection is, simply, "They must be
funny." It would be nice if more of them were.) And so the
mutations of American politics as shown in its cartoons must
be searched for in other pages than these; the curtain falls
somewhere around the toothy-drawings-of-Teddy-Roosevelt
period. Thus the unamused editor eliminates the few in-

Review of *Cartoon Cavalcade* edited by Thomas Craven, *Politics*,
May 1944. Reprinted by permission.

teresting political cartoonists of our own time—notably Fitz-patrick—altogether.

Comic strips are not well represented and those that get in are poorly arranged; the last half of the book is almost completely given over to work from the *New Yorker,* with occasional interruptions by Skeezix or Blondie, who seem a bit out of place. The differences between the closed worlds of each type of cartoon are profound; and had each been included in a separate section, we might have been permitted to see how the newspaper strip, which began with comic intentions, turned into a device for relating somewhat cretinous stories of romantic adventure, Mcfaddenesque solemnity, or of pseudo-scientific repetitions—usually turned out with a nice eye for sadomasochist effects. How did we ever get from Foxy Grandpa to Pruneface? It is a question that would no doubt fail to amuse Mr. Craven. But then Mr. Craven believes that our cartoons are what they are because Americans are a wholesome, fun-loving people.

The volume also contains three long essays by the editor— "lucid, gay, and civilized talk," says the dust-jacket. Three examples of Mr. Craven's lucidity, gaiety, and advanced state of social culture follow. "Phil May was a scream." "The intellectuals were strange souls who had lost their moorings. . . . They talked of Proust, Joyce, and Freud, of Picasso, Gertrude Stein, and other nonessentials. . . . The intellectuals were lost because they had no sense of humor." Best of all, though, is this: "The closest approach to the French acceptance of sex appeal appeared in the drawings which Nell Brinkley used to make for the *New York Evening Journal.*"

Cartoon Cavalcade is all too painfully reminiscent of a scrapbook to which some thoughtful but none too discriminating cartoon-lover—one with a well-nourished mania for preservation—has devoted many happy hours with scissors and paste. But with scissors and paste only.

Magazine Rack

Few readers of *Partisan Review* are likely to belong to that small but valiant coterie which takes its cue from *College English,* the official organ of the National Council of English Teachers. Its February number contains (along with more representative articles, such as "The Preterite-Present Verbs of Present-Day English") an article in which a Miss Winifred Lynskey gives Mr. John Crowe Ransom a rather rough going over. This may be worth a little attention.

Mr. Ransom, Miss Lynskey believes, falls into "serious inaccuracies," is a thoroughgoing Platonist, and is frequently guilty of wishing to "prove a point [rather] than be right." She is particularly repelled by the handling A. E. Housman receives from the critic. Ransom's "destruction" of the poem, in which Housman's deceased lightfoot lads and rose-lipt maidens load the poet's heart with rue, is accomplished, she feels, by an excess of literal analysis, and is, moreover, "inept" and "erroneous." It strikes me that here Miss Lynskey is less troubled by Ransom's strategies than by a desire to provide her own twenty-four sheet for a poem that is badly in need of it. Ransom's pertinacious dissection of the poem, on the other hand, reminds one somewhat of a Heidelberg encyclopedist reviewing a package of Tums.

Miss Lynskey will have none of Ransom's theory that Milton, in a publicity-seeking mood, deliberately wrote "Lycidas" as an irregular pastoral elegy. "I do not recall that Dryden, Addison, and Johnson, however they may have been

Partisan Review 9 (Spring 1944). Reprinted by permission.

irritated by some qualities of Milton, were disturbed by the ten unrhymed lines," says Miss Lynskey. "[The] irregularity does not seem to have disturbed many people in the last three hundred years." This is a new kind of tone for this type of argument—"No one else has ever complained before about my rooms not being warm enough, Mr. Ransom. I've been running this place for thirty years, and never *once* have I heard a word of complaint about the lumps in the mashed potatoes." But then this is an indescribably mixed-up fight.

When Miss Lynskey moves in for the kill, Ransom's "Shakespeare at Sonnets" makes the shooting easy; for this essay, which Miss Lynskey informs us is one that "Mr. Ransom's friends urged him not to publish," strings together a considerable aggregation of blunders. Lack of space and a wave of ennui forbid a summary of Miss Lynskey's extensive exposures of Mr. Ransom's contradictions; but she leaves little doubt that Ransom's friends, in urging him to suppress "Shakespeare at Sonnets," were giving him sound advice. It is an essay in which contrarieties and fixed ideas arrive early and work overtime; yet it scarcely sums up Ransom. But then Miss Lynskey is here gathering only the best wood for her hatchet.

With the little magazines, Mr. Ransom's own *Kenyon Review,* after its valuable Henry James number, disgorges a winter offering in the shape of four poems by Genevieve Taggard. This would seem to be too many. Surely the *Saturday Review of Literature* people are irritably biting their lips at having to see these verses published in other pages than their own.

> Hush new child, how
> Give you good love?
> (You now so new.)

writes Miss T., and continues:

> (Hush, children, while mother sings.)

As if to make up for this, the *Kenyon* prints a distinguished new poem by Allen Tate; several extracts from Gide's Journals (on Valéry, Claudel, and Proust) in an admirable translation by F. W. Dupee, which leave one unsatisfied only by the brevity of the selections; and a bright exegetical piece by C. G. Wallis on Cocteau's *Le Sang d'un Poète*.

View, with its December number, is well out of the little magazine class; it has become a Fifty-seventh Street edition of a ritzier *Cue,* mixing Surrealism with page after page of gallery notices and full-page *Vogue*-like ads for *White Flame* ("a breathtaking new perfume by Helena Rubinstein . . . to set his heart on fire") and for *Shocking Radiance,* Schiaparelli's new scent, plugged by a Dalí drawing. In spite of its frequent foolishness and its well-heeled *enfant terrible* posturings, I should be sorry to see *View* come to an end. Once banned by the Post Office, the December issue is now permitted to go through the mails again, and persons in far-off Wichita and Salt Lake City may read a poem on pink paper by Charles Henri Ford, examine some *National Geographic*–like photographs of underground caverns, and fail to finish a noisy contribution by Nicolas Calas. "Uncreative, second-rate minds these modern herologists!" shouts Mr. Calas, dipping into his well-stocked exclamation-point supply, "—incapable of understanding either the situation of the masses or the feelings of the individual!"

Things are quieter in the pages of *Horizon,* which still arrives each month from London—a professional, serious, balanced job. Recent issues contained some excellent articles, such as Rudolph Friedmann's psychoanalytic study of Kierkegaard, Stephen Spender's comment on the humanist tradition in German letters, and a report on Soviet life by a Polish journalist. However, *Horizon* might profit by recalling Mr. Connolly's pre-blitz spirit of irreverence. The Winter issue of *Accent* has a good Cummings poem, and devotes the bulk of its space to a piece by Richard Levin and Charles Shattuck, arguing close Homeric parallels in Joyce's *Dubliners.* Now that Joyce is safely buried, the publications of the Modern Language Association should be interested. A number of new magazines have recently appeared: the *Quarterly Review of Literature,* introducing a new note—a purple cover; Dwight Macdonald's *Politics;* a critical journal, the *American Bookman;*

Norman Macleod's *Maryland Quarterly;* and a mimeographed publication from California called *Circle,* enclosing Henry Miller. A number of other little magazines still function. Some of these perform the not uninteresting feat of assembling examples of criticism, poems, *and* stories of an exact degree of intellectual emaciation. This is not so easy a trick to bring off.

The reading of Kay Boyle's last novel induced in Mr. Edmund Wilson a sharp nostalgia for *transition* and *This Quarter*. It is a nostalgia that is currently stirring in many a literary bosom. (A number of the current little magazines would make one nostalgic for the *Yellow Book*.) Some intellectuals have not been content to limit themselves to the boundaries of this understandable response, but threaten at any moment to sigh longingly for the pleasant days of Mr. Coolidge, Sacco and Vanzetti, and Miss Millay's middle period. Yet the sense of fresh explorations perpetually going forward, the dissidence, the experimentation, above all the international spirit that animated the little magazines of the twenties, were of great importance. They survive only in a few caves here and there; and even the occupants of these underground hideouts have about them an air of overcharged desperation and a cultivated awareness that they are functioning with little help from those who appear to themselves as colleagues.

Most of the gifted editors of our time are dead or have assigned themselves roles in disappearing acts—Ford (Ford Madox, not Charles Henri), Margaret Anderson, Harriet Monroe; have given up editing (Eliot, Wyndham Lewis); or are wanted by the Allied police force (Pound). As for writers, a whole generation of "promising talents" examines its graying hairs and pouchy eyes in the cubicles of the O.W.I., the Time and Life Building, and in the scenario department of MGM. Many of them have not only succeeded in making complete adaptions to these realms, but have reconditioned them into closed worlds of value.

I have said little about the fiction and poetry in the new magazines. Most of these offerings are repeat performances from the recent past's extended run of creative stalemate and debility. There is a good deal to be said against the intellectual product of the twenties; yet those writers who established themselves in that period, and who still exist, reminding us occasionally of creatures from another age—Cummings, Eliot, Stevens, Williams, etc.—remain our most gifted avant-garde contributors. The competition from those who followed is a sporadic affair only. If that was a Wasteland and they were the Lost Generation, then what is this moldy milieu in which we find ourselves; and what are we?

Movie Notes

"Honesty is the best policy," is a reliable thematic standby of Hollywood that turns up again, feeble but resolute, as the substance of Mr. Preston Sturges's *Hail the Conquering Hero,* a dishonest, unfunny, a-human "comedy" that works like a miner in a landslide trying to look honest, to be funny, and to seem "human." The effort is carried à la Frank Capra, whom Mr. Sturges increasingly resembles; a little more of the sentimental in his next script and a role for Walter Brennan in it and the two men will be about as indistinguishable as Fox Movietone News and MGM's News of the Day.

In a farce, a character forced to play a role that humiliates and torments him is sure to arouse high merriment; if his antagonists are six heroic Marines (cheers) who are animated by a desire to see him restored to his mother, the finished production is practically in the cans. To add to the fun, Mr. Sturges has embellished his young hero with a bad case of hay fever, that hilarious ailment, and saves his greatest flourish of energy for a homecoming sequence that features such novel laugh-getters as two bands playing at once, endless cut-in shots of Franklin Pangborn mopping his brow and looking harried, and the greatest array of stock-pattern small-town types I have ever seen crammed into one movie. Sturges's manic handling of Raymond Walburn as the excitable mayor of the town would be embarrassing in a junior high school operetta. But perhaps the most offensive aspect of *Hail the Conquering Hero* is the wallowing self-congratulatory air with

Partisan Review 9 (Fall 1944). Reprinted by permission.

which Sturges embraces his two-faced relationship to his material. His witless exploitation and *pretended* kidding of a sadistic Marine with a mother fixation, for example, is perfectly balanced by a cinema mother who might have come off the top of a box of Martha Washington candy. Sturges's strategy is to fortify every cliché in the book, while his slapstick, unconvincingly masquerading as satire, thuds and thumps and never runs down.

What little of the hideousness and horror of the war that Hollywood has eyedroppered into its releases has been received by audiences with marked distaste; the shying-away from war films—or for that matter anything even remotely touching on reality—has become so sharply felt at the box-office that the new production schedules call for more and more "comedies," musicals, and uplift pieces. The motion picture industry's most relished statement on the war, so far as audiences are concerned, is no doubt to be found in the cretinous gagging of *Hail the Conquering Hero.* It has been enormously successful.

Though it is true that an actor portraying the twenty-eighth president of the United States unquestionably appears in Mr. Zanuck's Technicolored *Wilson,* it is more to the point, I think, to regard it as a musical picture—somewhat in the tradition of those films with Alice Faye or Betty Grable, in which a song-and-dance vaudevillian is tenderly chronicled from lowly tank-circuit endeavors to final achievement on the Big Time. Music is, indeed, the *subject* of *Wilson,* its garish figure in the carpet. A trumpet might very well appear on the main title. According to the advertisements for the film, eighty-seven "beloved songs" are played or sung in *Wilson;* and though I got the impression that there were even more than eighty-seven, it serves no purpose to question Mr. Zanuck's figure. For three-quarters of this long and soporific picture, which cost three-and-a-half million dollars, an approximation of history carries on a losing battle with vocal, orchestral, or band renditions of "Put on Your Old Gray Bonnet," "Hail to the Chief," "Over There," "I Didn't Raise My Boy to Be a Soldier," and the eighty-three others, most of them executed by one of the most ear-shattering brass sections of all time. Vocal choruses of "By the Light of the Silvery Moon," as rendered by the Wilson family around the parlor piano, are more searchingly documented than the First World War, which is brushed off rather hurriedly by way of some old newsreel clips showing Douglas Fairbanks, Mary Pickford, and Marie Dressler drumming up business for the Liberty Bond Drive, and quick glances at farmerettes, General Pershing, and parades. From the film's opening scene, a tender slow pan shot of the Princeton campus, until Wilson leaves the White House, its hero rushed about to football and baseball games (episodes which perform the double duty of establishing Wilson as a not untypical American lover of sport, and giving the band a chance to play good and loud), to a variety theater (where some more music can be dragged in and where Wilson's reactions to Lew Dockstader and Eddie Foy point up his zest for the theater), and to such Sousa-havens as political rallies.

Somewhere around Reel Nine, *Wilson* settles down to (a) convincing its audience of the nobility of America's aims in fighting World War I, (b) absolving the American people of guilt in the League of Nations fight, and (c) converting that tragic affair into a matter of personalities, with Wilson as messiah and Henry Cabot Lodge as villain. Such a significant figure in Wilson's life as Colonel House is seen so briefly that if your eyes leave the screen for a moment, you are apt to miss him entirely. Most of the other historical figures dart on and off with the speed of waterbugs. Wilson's own chilly, complex, eccentric, theological-seminary characteristics are scrapped for more genial and photogenic ones; he becomes a family man who occasionally has to pay a visit to the office to straighten out a few business matters. As for what was responsible for the economic and political nightmare of the period 1914–1920, there is only one explanation: Germany.

William Carlos Williams

William Carlos Williams's first full-size book of verse since his *Complete Collected Poems, 1906–1938* sharply defines a figure whose position in American writing is one of the most curious of the time. This New Jersey pediatrician and part-time writer is that nearly unique phenomenon—an American man of letters whose fiction and poetry can confront each other without embarrassment. His work is the product of an original sensibility, equally at home with prose narrative or verse.

We expect "modernist" poetry to be "neglected," of course, and when our snug expectations are now and then jolted some of us are apt to feel a momentary and perhaps snobbish uneasiness. But the absence of a wider appreciation for Dr. Williams's fiction remains merely puzzling. Anyone who admires Hemingway and Sherwood Anderson, for instance, ought to look up his first two collections of stories, *The Knife of the Times* and *Life Along the Passaic River*. They should be warned, however, that they will find something quite different from either Hemingway or Anderson. Williams's sense of the exact takes him far beyond or apart from their "disillusionment," and he is about as sentimental as a court reporter.

With only two exceptions, his twenty volumes—poems, short stories, novels, journals, history—have been brought out by avant-garde publishers in tiny editions or by the hardly big-league New Directions. Commercial publishers seem to care nothing for him. Most anthologists include him but rep-

Review of *The Wedge* by William Carlos Williams, *New York Times Book Review*, February 11, 1945. Copyright © 1945 by The New York Times Company. Reprinted by permission.

resent him badly. Today's fashions in poetry have made his continued devotion to Imagist doctrines look more unfashionable than ever.

Yet the best of these poems in *The Wedge,* with their oblique and unceremonious rhythms, their celebrations of the commonplace—concise, sharp, tough-minded, and clean, like all his mature work—resist the compulsions of fashion. Williams has always used the American language in poetry with a strictness that makes such a writer as Carl Sandburg, for instance, sound merely wispy and soft; and he continues to find, in areas that many poets might dismiss as unrewarding, values and distinctions that only his methods of observation reveal.

Everything he sees, he sees with fresh eyes; and that is one reason why some of his work is simply flat, primitive, or ecstatically shrill. His capacity for discrimination lags behind his gift for keeping his eyes rooted on the object. When he stares at an "idea," we can only wish he might have managed not to: an out-of-focus effect usually sets in. His unsynchronized leaps into the arenas of formal ideas have always caused his admirers embarrassed dismay. (He has provided another one in his introduction to *The Wedge* when he says: "Let the metaphysical take care of itself, the arts have nothing to do with it.")

The poetry is another matter. In such poems as "Burning the Christmas Greens," "Eternity," "A Vision of Labor," "The Semblables," and "The Hounded Lovers," he produces some of the magically intense effects we have come to expect of him. And the pictorial precision of a poem like "The Yellow Chimney" works on us in the same way as some of the wonderful early photographs of Atget and Stieglitz.

Recent Books of Verse

Five Young American Poets, 1944 is the third of a series of volumes that New Directions began to issue in 1940. The first two helped to introduce and advance the reputations of such men as Karl Shapiro, John Berryman, and Randall Jarrell; and both of the earlier books were considerably more lively than this one. The poets included in the 1944 volume are Jean Garrigue, Tennessee Williams, Eve Merriam, John Frederick Nims, and an Ecuadorian, Alejandro Carrión. Each of them is represented by some forty pages of verse.

In the interest of the good-neighbor policy, let us look first at Señor Carrión's work. This "foremost younger poet" of Ecuador is described in a note as "earthy, direct and intense," and we are also informed that his poetry is composed under "great excitement . . . its first form is its final form." An examination of the poems seems to reinforce the truth of this account. They are obviously freed from the deliberations and anxieties of revision. Carrión writes pale, sentimental proletarian verse of the sort that at one time was very prevalent in Communist party circles—verse dealing with "the uncheckable fever of laborers" and "red roses [that] flower on the workers' breasts." In his non-proletarian moments only the sentimentality remains. Mr. Dudley Fitts, who is a very capable translator, has, I think, wasted his time in getting Car-

---

Review of *Five Young American Poets, Third Series* and *The Summer Landscape* by Rolfe Humphries, *New York Times Book Review,* June 17, 1945. Copyright © 1945 by The New York Times Company. Reprinted by permission.

rión into English. Ecuador, though a small country, surely has something more agreeable in the way of young poetic talent than this.

Miss Eve Merriam is a kind of part-time "social" poet, too. She writes brief topical verses for *PM* (not included here) and her viewpoint is a "poetic" variant of the one that publication usually sets forth. Her originality, such as it is, consists of plowing under certain words—mainly "a," "an," and "the"— as much as she can. As a result we have:

> Wife worries last-minute speck of lint
> from flawless couch; husband, her host, is mute,
> conversation corked till cloud of company
> shall swirl, powdered and plumed,
> into the pregnant room.

Miss Jean Garrigue's very personal and metaphysical poems are probably the most satisfactory exhibits in this collection. Although there are some irritating lah-de-dah disfigurations here and there, and although her ear is far from sharp, she is worth reading. Her "Waking . . ." and "Journey to the Last Station" have very good things in them.

Not so much can be said for Tennessee Williams, who blends a diffuse vagueness with a state of excitation the source of which remains decidedly unclear. The following lines suggest his quality:

> O Mother of Blue Mountain boys
> come to the screen-door calling
> Come in, come in!
> before it gets dreadfully dark and hailstones fall
> as big as goose-eggs nearly!

Even Señor Carrión's "first drafts" have nothing to compare with Mr. Williams's productions, not to mention his sizable hailstones.

John Frederick Nims, whose ventures have won him a number of prizes, has a more knowing sense of form than any of his companions here. He aims, so he says, at a "definite and Mozartean structure." But I am afraid that even with all his sophistication he has actually given us something which more closely resembles a somewhat disjointed potpourri: the progressions of his verse suggest a speeded-up medley more than anything by the composer of "Eine Kleine Nachtmusik."

Mr. Nims is fond of writing poems "about" objects, institutions and places—some of their titles are "Poolroom," "Magazine Stand," "Colt Automatic," "Slums," "Penny Arcade," "Seashore," and "Dollar Bill." Each one provides the poet with a loose point of departure for a prolonged and rather mechanical assembly-job of over-elaborate metaphors.

Most of Mr. Nims's poems are conglutinations of analogies, emblems, and the figurative that might have been modeled on the exact opposite of the Imagists' doctrine: "Use no superfluous word; don't mix abstractions with the concrete; avoid unrevealing adjectives." Hart Crane and a few others partially solved a rhetorical problem superficially resembling the one facing Nims.

After all this, Rolfe Humphries's third book of poems, *The Summer Landscape,* comes as a most refreshing change. Unlike the *Five Young American Poets,* Humphries is completely aware of his limitations, always competent and readable, quiet, shrewd, witty, and deeply suspicious of inflated effects. His chief affinities are with Herrick, Housman, and Yeats. Humphries prefaced an earlier book of his with this sentence: "A minor art needs to be hard, condensed, and durable." At its best, his work is still minor, hard, and condensed; and I think the very best of it may be as durable, at least, as a superior grade of aluminum, the surface of which almost all of his poems—good, bad, and indifferent—strongly suggest. "The Exiles," "La Belle Dame Sans Merci," "From My Travels," "The Summer Landscape," and "They Talk about the Weather" are among the best things he has written; and "For My Ancestors," which deals with the Welsh, is excellent light satirical verse of the sort that almost no one, in these days, seems capable of writing.

An Academic Bohemia

Mr. Hoffman and Mr. Allen have taken a first-class subject and produced a result that may compassionately be termed third-rate. This study of the "little" magazines, the first full-length account to appear, should offer illumination of a sort to those who have never looked at, subscribed to, read, or written for them. Probably the chief distinction of the book, concerned as it is with the magazines that first expounded every advanced idea and technical innovation of the last thirty years, is that its authors should sound as though they had just returned, rather limply, from red-penciling a C plus on a theme about freshman hazing. When they rally from this state, they approach their subject with all the undiscriminating enthusiasm of a phrenologist for cranial irregularities.

To put one's finger on the places Mr. Hoffman and Mr. Allen go wrong would entail a wearisome pointing at page after page. Without any general theories of culture, fresh or borrowed, to give meaning to their sequence of events, the careers of the magazines they chronicle with varying degrees of thoroughness but with a steady naïveté—*Poetry, Blast,* the *Little Review,* the *Criterion, This Quarter,* the *Dial, Hound and Horn, Partisan Review,* and all the others—are only interesting phenomena. A good many muffin-headed notions about avant-garde publications are weighed here and found decidedly worth keeping. The impulse behind the origins of the little magazine in English (the authors have patriotically re-

Review of *The Little Magazine: A History and a Bibliography* by Frederick J. Hoffman, Charles Allen, and Carolyn F. Ulrich, *The Nation,* August 31, 1946. Reprinted by permission.

stricted themselves to periodicals in this tongue) was one symptom of the cultural lag that slowed down the importation of "modern" nineteenth-century attitudes, of which the most heroic exponents were Flaubert, Rimbaud, and Baudelaire. (Hoffman and Allen have a reference to Rimbaud—as a contributor to Mr. Laughlin's Poet of the Month series.) Other predecessors, here at home, were Henry James and Henry Adams, with their lips curled at the mention of local editorial opinion. But Hoffman and Allen give us, instead of roots and continuity, the familiar introductory story of Harriet Monroe, in 1912, brooding about *Poetry* in Chicago, an intent modernist Adam. They can later enlist their gifts as goggled tourists to string together the following set of words: "[*Poetry*] carries on today with the same high spirit and intelligence that has made its past record so brilliant."

The authors have gifts for relieving a reader's irritation with even finer comic touches. I would not willingly keep back these few examples, among their best:

> The poet's trumpeting for a political and military cause may very well improve the quality of radio and cinema fare.

> Indeed, there is much truth in Pearl Buck's observation that our literature has always been regional . . .

> The poetry of Herbert Read has always been a credit to left-wing literature.

If *The Little Magazine* were merely a foolish or accurately academic affair, it would be easy to be merely unkind. But Hoffman and Allen have not even exploited the meager source material available. They have remained undefiled by the spirit of such lively personal accounts as those of Pound, Wyndham Lewis, McAlmon, Cowley, Margaret Anderson, and Ford Madox Ford. Some of these, along with pieces that are first-rate contributions, by Ford, Clement Greenberg, and Parker Tyler, are not even included in their list of sources. (Pound's article on the little magazine, in the *English Journal*, tells more in 6 pages than our present historians do in 230.)

Their vigorously affirmative attitude toward errors has made possible, on page 208, the compilation of a charming little treasury. They deftly manage to misspell the name of Lincoln Kirstein's novel, remark that *"The Hound and Horn* did not discover any noteworthy writers," thus confidently settling the hash of James Agee, and refer to a mysterious *Hound and Horn* contributor named "Ellery Larsson." Going on the reasonably safe assumption that this is not Ellery Queen, I take it to be Raymond E. F. Larsson in one of his frequent appellative rearrangements; but with Hoffman and Allen one is never sure.

Their method of historical sequence, combined with a tasteless eclecticism—the editor of the *Midland,* John T. Frederick, gets more searching attention than T. S. Eliot, Wyndham Lewis, and F. M. Ford as editors, combined—can only result in disconnected accounts of "tendencies" and the destinies of individual magazines. The "changes" thus revealed are mere links in the "progress" of literature. This may enchant progress-enthusiasts, who are welcome to their enchantment. Unmentioned, and perhaps unmentionable, is the key issue of Bohemianism, which provided the main scaffolding for the little magazine, and Bohemianism's bizarre convolutions from a serious origin to its dead end today in professional Bohemianism and the warmed-over "avant-garde" productions of—dare one invite the anger of *PM?*— Mr. Patchen. In the same way that a little magazine becomes dull without a program as well as taste and brains—most of those published today serve goulashes of "modernism" and the academic—so does a history of them.

Miss Ulrich is a reliable bibliographer and her section is valuable, reasonably complete, and mainly accurate; its usefulness would have been enhanced by a listing of the number of issues brought out by each magazine. The index, in keeping with the text, is poor.

Moons, Nested Like Tawny Birds

These poems by the late Mary Webb (author of *Precious Bane*), who died in 1927, were recently discovered among her husband's papers. Walter de la Mare admires them; but then, Yeats admired Dorothy Wellesley's.

Nothing is harder to warm up to than the dated language of the recent past; a third-rate Elizabethan or someone Swift attacked seemed, in comparison, charm itself. Mrs. Webb, however, lovingly preserved a closetful of all the "poetic" odds and ends thrown out by Pound and his followers in a historic and badly needed housecleaning. Her poems have the look of objects no longer very fresh and not even decorative; Victorian but not antique, they would go well with the least appealing varieties of Staffordshire dogs, cuckoo clocks, volumes bound in red plush, button-boxes decorated with the likenesses of prominent suffragettes. The late Victorians found the world they lived in to be distant, inadmissible, and unrewarding as a "poetical" source; and their poems emerged, rather too gratuitously, from a dream-world. Mrs. Webb's poems, written some years later, are a dream about that dream-world. They are, that is, anachronisms following in the wake of a misapprehension.

Most frequently they are scenic, and the scene is one selected by a contented Sunday painter who always visits the same acre. The season is spring; nature is kind; seldom in any

Review of *Fifty-One Poems* by Mary Webb, *New York Times Book Review*, November 9, 1947. Copyright © 1947 by The New York Times Company. Reprinted by permission.

verse I know do people plant seeds so often or do buds burst
with such persistant and cheerful regularity:

> Little flowers with golden eyes
> Lift their heads in sweet surprise

Turning the pages, to discover what loosens "the last leaf," we
discover that it is "The Breath Divine."

Her poems are dotted with moons that nest like "tawny
birds," stars are "steadfast," and there are a lot of peculiar
verbs of the order of "dwelleth," "hummeth" (a bee does
this), and "lieth." When these stanzas are glad they are very
glad:

> Pink dawns are flung across the world
> So welcome, life

But when they are sad, they are quick to engage such gloomy
and dusk-haunted props as ruined castles, where something
or someone referred to as "Grim Foreboding" speaks briefly
in gothic tones.

Unhappy Expatriate

Henry Miller, onetime Paris expatriate, *vieux-terrible* of long standing, and author of *Tropic of Cancer,* returned to the country of his birth, the United States, as World War II began to make its appearance on the face of Europe. Miller has been living here ever since, none too happily, apparently, for he entertains an attitude toward his native land not unlike that usually reserved for a public dump. In Paris, Miller's paper-backed novels became, for literate American soldiers during the war, what *Ulysses* had been for American tourists of the Continent in the twenties, and they established him, in Miller's own gratified words, as "one accused of employing obscene language more freely and abundantly than any other living writer in the English language."

Tropic of Cancer, with its inspired rhetorical flights that interrupted the adventures of a group of fantastically prurient and down-at-the-heel expatriates, seemed, at the time, enormously fresh and appropriate. The book appeared to come out of genuine emotion and need. But Miller's recent works, which make steady and annual appearances, have been largely journalistic and autobiographical miscellanies, and progressively more windy and tedious. *Remember to Remember* continues this trend.

Isaac Rosenfeld has remarked that Miller is a man on a holiday from taste. By now the holiday has developed into a

Review of *Remember to Remember* by Henry Miller, *New York Times Book Review,* November 30, 1947. Copyright © 1947 by The New York Times Company. Reprinted by permission.

protracted retirement, with all of its attendant atrophies. For Miller the world is a mural, with everything oversize. Things, institutions, nations, and human beings are viewed as devoid of complexity or contradictions; they are only subjects for attack, the more furious the better, or praise, usually lavish. The people Miller admires (who I hope will not forgive him for referring to them as "little people") are blown up by this author to mural size, with only their more attractive features showing. The handwriting of one of Miller's friends, for instance, is not something that offers possibilities for coherent description, but is, quite simply, "the most amazing, and perhaps the most incredible, handwriting imaginable." Miller gives the game away, however, by reproducing a sample of it, thus indicating that he has apparently been shielded from very many examples of penmanship.

Three of the pieces in *Remember to Remember* are appreciations of artist friends—Varda, Beauford Delaney, and Abraham Rattner. Miller's tone here is that of a publicity man winding up a campaign on Leonardo, Rembrandt, and the Post-Impressionists. It is hard to take Miller with any seriousness at all after his judgment on Rattner. This artist, as a colorist, he says, "has gone beyond Picasso, Matisse, [and] Roualt."

One takes for granted Miller's awareness of the extent of decay in our civilization and his hatred of war. But the rhetoric that fizzes and rumbles from his anarchistic pacifism has a strident echo after the utterances of the men in whose tradition I take him to be writing—Thoreau, Debs, and Randolph Bourne. The clarity, passion, and humanity of their absolutism give way, in Miller, to a spleenish tubthumpery, anvil-handed irony, and an opportunism of argument that must be read to be believed. Miller seems, indeed, at the mercy of any idea at all, so long as it is sufficiently monolithic, and in his opinion shocking enough, for his use.

"What do I find wrong with America? Everything." He can quote, with approval, Péguy's wonderful strictures on debasement in the modern world, but provide a loophole for France (an object of praise) to escape Péguy's damnation. He can marvelously advocate the detachment of such men as Lao-tse and St. Francis (to Miller, "men of God are joyous men"), while flourishing the most full-blown Bohemian orthodoxy of the time.

"The critics and the reviewers, the army of hired prostitutes who blow as the wind blows," Miller writes, ". . . will deluge me with insults, they will say that I am warped and twisted, that my ideas are subversive, that I am a traitor and a renegade." I should dislike disappointing Miller, who I suspect is personally most genial; but it is hard to find him warped and twisted at all, but merely a sort of Cassandra-produced Town Meeting of the Air. His ideas are not so much subversive, whatever that is, but only stale, fitful, and without complexity, and both his indictments and hosannas sound a good deal like the extremities to which radio advertising is committed. And if Miller is a renegade from anything, it is only from discrimination, from insight, and, necessarily, from art.

Diminishing Pastures

Norman Macleod is an American who has published three books of poems. This, his fourth, although its subtitle would have it otherwise, is a very incomplete selection of seventeen years of his work. Marxism, regionalism, and a deep sense of unease were the major and rather disjunctive elements of his earlier poetry; remnants of the first two are still mistily evident, but his uneasiness has developed into a state of panicky ferment. Macleod once wrote prolifically and with a kind of willed simplicity; the most likable poem in this volume is an early one of only three lines:

> There was a girl we all remembered:
> Her face was a scarlet
> Spider lily, and she feathered the grass with screams.

These days he writes little, and with a kind of willed intricacy. He has always seemed, on the basis of his tensions, to be at rock bottom a poet of the ingrown ego, although his early work was usually straining toward a place in the crowd—toward Mr. MacLeish's public poetry or at a point beyond it. Travel, political observations on strikes, Spain, life in the Southwest, were recurring topics. It is now difficult to say just what the centers are toward which Macleod converges. Many of the new poems are pieced together with sequences of ap-

---

Review of *A Man in Midpassage: Collected Poems, 1939–1947* by Norman Macleod and *Never A Greater Need* by Walter Benton, *New York Times Book Review*, April 4, 1948. Copyright © 1948 by The New York Times Company. Reprinted by permission.

parently intended conceits; and I have tried, with more so-
lemnity than I find temperamentally agreeable, to discover
what animates them.

"It may be better," Macleod writes in a typical passage, "the
curtain call carry the rushes of its unperfected film." Rushes
are, in this context, I take it, not stemmed plants, but devel-
oped negatives of motion-picture takes. The passage is thus
far beautifully tautological. A curtain call is a term of the
legitimate theater. Rushes are, of course, necessarily "unper-
fected"; they are unedited, uncut, unscored—subject to all
manner of processes and corrections before they are "per-
fect" prints, ready for exhibition. Then, too, how can a cur-
tain call "carry" anything? Rushes are carried by can-
carriers—mostly boys or young men employed, in places
where movies are produced, for conveying film from place to
place. Is Macleod suggesting that these people be replaced by
"the curtain call"? He says "it may be better." What the "it"
refers to I cannot fathom.

Imprecisions and crude ambiguities of this kind pervade
the book. Frequently they are joined by alliterative embar-
rassments. A line I expect to rattle in my head until we are
atomized: "Their laundered limbs lifted with love."

The verse of Walter Benton presents no such perplexities
as Mr. Macleod's. Children could read it with ease; and I
suppose many of them do. His first book, *This Is My Beloved,*
published in 1943, has gone into printing after printing and is
as staple an item in bookstores as Robert Frost or Mrs. Rom-
bauer's cookbook. Benton has a vast audience among under-
graduates, the more sensitive chorus girls, and among thou-
sands of people who otherwise take no interest at all in
modern poetry. But then Mr. Benton is not a modern poet.

Never a Greater Need, like its predecessor, is one long boy-
hood dream of eroticism, breathtakingly silly, easier to read
than a tabloid but a good deal emptier and less moving. Mr.
Benton is fond of three dots (. . .) to keep his poems moving
along like paste out of a tube; if Nick Kenny rewrote the Song
of Solomon, *Never a Greater Need* might be the result. These
lines suggest the tone: "All your incomparable body laughs to
my touch," "This then is you . . . tender-eyed, nineteen . . .

mine." Moving out of the bedroom, Mr. Benton is not much different from any other disciple of Norman Corwin: "This poem is for . . . the little nobody people. . . ."

I enjoyed the book enormously though—almost as much as *The Five Little Peppers* or a wonderful book the title of which I forget: it was bound in pink cloth and published by the authoress, a kindly old Southern lady who wrote nothing but sonnets and who addressed them all to her pet dog, a St. Bernard.

His Preservation of Himself as a
Twenties Literary Expatriate

"Don't tell me you love me," an old Spanish proverb goes, "show me you love me." But for years now Henry Miller has been *telling* us—about his feelings, his ideas, the ideas of other men. Actual demonstrations, the real thing, ceased a good many books back. Experience has always been enormously important to him (his flirtations with philosophy and mysticism have the flavor of some of the more rudimentary Haldiman-Julius Little Blue Books); but only his Brooklyn and Paris experiences furnished him with anything offering much in the way of demonstration, a fact that would seem to indicate his present location in California is, so far as his career is concerned, a poor one. The spontaneity and sense of the actual of the *Tropics* days have given way to the established literary man's chief occupational disease—the necessity of writing even when the well is dry, even when his language is, as it is in this new book of Miller's, of a sort the moths abandoned long ago: ". . . listlessly toying with the throngs of memory," "at this point a disturbing thought suddenly shattered his revery," "and then, like a knife gleam, there came a flash of memory," etc.

Miller's most recent works have been *telling*—exclamatory, bombastic, indiscriminate—that America is a sort of spiritual, ethical, and economic pig-wallow, that France is more wonderful than it was to Sisley Huddleston or the French steam-

Review of *The Smile at the Foot of the Ladder* by Henry Miller, *Tiger's Eye*, October 20, 1948.

108

ship lines, that it is impossible to find good bread in the United States, that his friends are spectacular and amazing personalities, hints that his own personality is perhaps not out of keeping with theirs, and that his experiences and insights, at the very least, border on the transcendental. His tone is that of a merchandiser—a merchandiser who never allows you to get too searching a look at what you are being talked into buying.

A considerable amount of Henry Miller's appeal—chiefly to the young of all ages who form his cult (their older brothers eagerly awaited new issues of the *American Mercury* under Mencken)—springs from his preservation of himself as a twenties literary expatriate, complete with standard personality fixtures, during a time of pervasive extinction of personality, willed and unwilled, among American writers. This act of preservation carries with it the vulgarity, not so much of one who endlessly debates whether to be fashionable or unfashionable, but one so overconcerned by individuality as a careerist necessity that he renders its functionings inoperative. Mr. Miller's hero in his new book is a clown ("my most intimate friends [look] upon me as a clown") who "had to assume the powers of a very special being with a very special gift." The word "assume" would seem to be important here. Miller's personality, and his continuing reputation, rest on the assumption, habitually self-reinformed, of himself as "a very special being with a very special gift." But artists are not, very often, messiahs with tight-rope acts. "I began," Miller writes in an afterword to his story, ". . . with the firm conviction that I had in me all there was to know about clowns and circuses. I wrote from line to line, blindly, not knowing what would come next." And though Miller is apparently asking in his story, "How can we be alive? How can we be happy? How can we be artists?," he cannot show us how; he cannot even tell us any more. It is a remarkably silly and boring little book; but probably anyone who began to write with "the firm conviction" that he had in him "all there was to know" about anything, or who wrote "from line to line, blindly," might tell us as little, and bore us as much.

Literature

Early American writing is a thin branch of the literature of seventeenth-century England, but with the important difference that the major concerns of those who settled the colonies were overwhelmingly religious. It is a literature largely given over to such matters as the relationship of church and state, the absolute sovereignty of God, biblical infallibility—a narrow religiosity the effects of which can still be felt in some contemporary writing, still tirelessly engaged in reacting against its distant influence. While the idea of human damnation and the vision of life as evil have produced some of the masterpieces of world literature, the authoritarian and dogmatic Calvinism of early New England, which stamped on almost every activity of mankind the mark of the devil, was scarcely hospitable to the production of works of art. It made room for pamphleteering, sermons, and for authorities on sin—for the fierce scolding of Cotton Mather, the remarkable and frequently brilliant sermons of Jonathan Edwards, most famous of Calvinism's champions, and for the vigorous and rebellious opponent of theocracy, Roger Williams.

While the earliest writers emphasized the ways of God to the exclusion of almost all other ways, their followers were increasingly devoted to the life of reason. Untouched by his Calvinist upbringings and frequently celebrated as the country's earliest figure of urbanity and cosmopolitanism, Benjamin Franklin was such a devotee, and one who excelled as a diplomat, politician, and economist as well as a writer. His

From *The American Guide* (New York: Hastings House, 1949).

Autobiography is still widely read. Franklin is perhaps the most important individual to span the period leading up to the Revolutionary War, a period most notable for its politics, oratory, and pamphleteering. Thomas Paine, with his *Common Sense,* made a reputation as a fiery advocate of American Independence. Patriotic versifiers were busily at work; best remembered are Philip Freneau, the first American poet of talent, who brought bitter satire to the national cause, and Joel Barlow. The towering reputation of Thomas Jefferson is in part due to his writings, among them the Declaration of Independence, as well as to his statemanship.

It was not, however, until the early nineteenth century that the country produced a writer of outstanding imaginative gifts. Washington Irving's *Knickerbocker's History of New York* has been called "the first American book that stood solidly on its own feet." Irving, representative of a new and aristocratic generation that celebrated elegance, romanticism, and the picturesque, though a man poorly equipped for understanding either himself or his world—of expansion, middle-class revolution, and industrial change—left, in *Rip Van Winkle, The Legend of Sleepy Hollow,* and *Knickerbocker's History,* still popular records of his flight into the legendary. It was a flight that was to be repeated by numerous writers that followed. Stimulated by the success of Scott's Waverly novels, James Fenimore Cooper discovered the Indian and served up the romantic myth of the American hinterland, employing devices of suspense that in their crudity foreshadowed the effects of Pearl White and the Lone Ranger. "Every time a Cooper person is in peril, and absolute silence is worth four dollars a minute," wrote Mark Twain, "he is sure to step on a dry twig." Nathaniel Hawthorne, saturated in the allegorical, in irony, and with a deep sense of evil, dramatized the Puritan tragedy as his forerunners had been unable to do. For it was only when Calvinism had begun to decline as a controlling force, apparently, that it could be put to creative use. It was Calvinism's appeal as a great fact of imagination, rather than its religiosity, that drew Hawthorne to brood on it for a lifetime and to produce four masterly novels, *The Scarlet Letter, The House of the Seven Gables, The Blithedale Romance,* and *The*

Marble Faun. But to the critics who have assessed American writers on the basis of extroversion and "involvement," Hawthorne is "a romancer of the twilight instead of the human heart," and "the extreme and finest expression of refined alienation from reality." Herman Melville, one of the most lacerated and savagely honest figures in our literature, has encountered similar treatment. In the author of *Moby-Dick*, such critics have been tireless in pointing out, there is too much hatred of life, too much meaningless suffering, too much escapism, symbolism, obscurity, bombast, Shakespearean rhetoric, too much awareness of human evil, too much that is inchoate and sordid, too much of doom and fatality. In recent years Melville and Hawthorne have come to be recognized as two of America's greatest novelists, and both have claimed wider audiences than ever before.

Melville's total disgust for the materialism and emptiness of his own time limited his public in his own lifetime in a way that the vigorously critical but serenely transcendental views of Ralph Waldo Emerson, however deeply they judged American realities, could never do. Though he was devoid of a tragic sense, there is an austerity and craftmanship that set Emerson apart from all the rest of the New England literary men of his time, except for Thoreau, whose arch-individualism, anarchism, and espousal of creativity single him out to many as the most modern of nineteenth-century writers. And while Thoreau was turning his back on the values of his countrymen, and while Edgar Allan Poe was creating new artistic values of his own and living out one of the most tragic of all among the many tragic lives of American artists, Walt Whitman, a walking anthology of affirmation and celebration, appeared to chant the inexhaustible glories of Democracy. No two figures could be less alike than Poe and Whitman, and they stand today as archetypes of many less important writers who followed. While Poe wrestled with his private and heartsick nightmares, marked by a pre-existentialist intensity and by guilt-ridden suffering, Whitman married extroversion to blank verse, drawing the citizens of the entire continent to him in his vision of the bright tomorrows promised by liberty, equality, and fraternity. With Whitman, the remnants of Calvinism fray out to nothing. Never before had the doctrine of the perfectibility of man enjoyed so assured and robust a celebrant.

Poles apart from Whitman and unknown to her own time, representing a sort of provincialism of the self, was Emily Dickinson, in whose verse emerged the finest voice and one of the most strongly defined personalities of the century. For the first time, the country had produced a writer who was completely an artist, capable of the purest communication of sensation and perception, one beyond the dominion of either ideas or rhetoric, and secure in the dominion of poetic ultimates.

While her reputation has steadily increased, an overhauling in taste has been less kind to five poets once strongly established and significant to their contemporaries—Oliver Wendell Holmes, John Greenleaf Whittier, James Russell Lowell, Henry Wadsworth Longfellow, and William Cullen Bryant. Today, the rather tame and Bostonian wit of Holmes, the Abolitionist fervor and idealism of Lowell, the impassioned democratic faith of Bryant, the old-fashioned Quakerism of Whittier, and the placid sentimentality of Longfellow have all merged in a general blur that obscures their individual works and personalities.

Noteworthy, if for no other reason than because of his position as the foremost Southern poet of the period, is Sidney Lanier, who attempted to blend music and language in his writings. Other Southern writers of the time include the scholarly and cultivated Hugh Legaré, the vigorous and prolific romantic novelist William Gilmore Simms, Augustus Longstreet, an early exponent of frontier humor, and John P. Kennedy, a neglected novelist who was influenced by his friend, Washington Irving.

Meanwhile, other novelists were discovering the great world of fact. Mark Twain, chief ornament of a long humorist tradition, offered his vision of the frontier, progressing in a score of books from the sparkling wit of *Innocents Abroad* to his masterpiece, *Huckleberry Finn,* to the disenchanted satire of his last years. Harriet Beecher Stowe pioneered in the propaganda novel with *Uncle Tom's Cabin.* William Dean Howells devoted himself to the novel of manners, Bret Harte to the mining camps, Joel Chandler Harris to Georgia plantation life, George W. Cable to romance in the Old South, Ambrose Bierce to impressive themes of the savage and the sardonic, Sara Orne Jewett to the New England past. Though Henry Adams's anonymous novel of Washington politics, *Democracy*, reveals a novelistic talent, it is in his autobiography, *The Education of Henry Adams*, his letters, and *Mont-Saint-Michel and Chartres*, a study of the nature of history through the meaning of the Middle Ages, that he is acclaimed today as one of the most distinguished minds of his time. With a greater awareness and sharper insight into the multiplicity of industrial society than any of his contemporaries, and with an unrivaled skepticism and wit, Adams never faltered in his search for the permanent and genuine. His description of his life as a failure is one of the major ironies in the records of self-evaluation.

From 1876 to his death in 1916, Henry James relieved fiction of its commitments to parochialism, crudity, and topicality by the publication of a succession of unmatched novels and stories, among them some of the few flawless works in American literature. In James's hands, fiction was charged with an artistry that could take its place with the fiction of France and England and Russia. The lesson of Henry James—at least the lesson of structure and tone—has been largely ignored by later generations of American novelists, whose adherence to the cult of raw material and autobiography has been noteworthy. In Edith Wharton, however, James had a devoted pupil and, in several of her best books, a brilliant one.

James was widely unread. The novelists who dominated the early years of the twentieth century found no easier an acceptance. But their difficulties lay in their outspoken insistence on a world of fact that post-Victorian sensibilities preferred to ignore. Their novels might have been the result of an outline drawn up to emphasize everything that their predecessors had left out, and to re-emphasize everything that those predecessors had touched on but lightly—the grossness of the physical world, sexuality, the corruption and debasement of a business society, the social consequences of the profit motive, the suffering of the poor—all accompanied by an onslaught against smugness, puritanism, and sentimentality. Most of the American naturalists, whose efforts were accompanied by the exposés of the "muckrakers" of business and politics—Lincoln Steffens, Ida Tarbell, Ray Stannard Baker among them—were to see America as a pigeonhole stuffed with problems. Robert Herrick rooted into feminism, the academic situation, labor. Upton Sinclair dealt with legal injustice, coal mining, the meatpackers, international politics. Jack London explored the Alaskan frontier, the South Seas, and Socialism. Frank Norris, deeply marinated in French naturalism, concerned himself with the city and the wheatfields. E. W. Howe, Hamlin Garland, and Henry B. Fuller proclaimed, in their novels, the first literary movement of the Middle West. Stephen Crane, a finer artist than any of these men, was a naturalist saved by poetry; his novels and stories of suffering and poverty are shot through with imagistic flashes and a feeling for texture none of his colleagues remotely apprehended.

The story of Theodore Dreiser's difficulties in launching his first novel, *Sister Carrie,* with his publishers burying copies of it in the basement, is frequently told to emphasize the hostility engendered by the new Naturalism. To the inheritors of the genteel tradition, it seemed a literature spawned in the basement, if not the sewer. With Dreiser, Naturalism was set forth in a style a moving-van might have conceived. "He is," Ludwig Lewisohn has said, "the worst writer of his eminence in the entire history of literature." Tasteless, brooding, sluggish, plodding, measuring life to a mechanistic pattern, Dreiser is nevertheless evaluated as one of the greatest American novelists, and *Sister Carrie, Jennie Gerhardt, An American Tragedy,* and the Cowperwood novels retain whatever vitality they may have because Dreiser builds a broad, real, varied, doomed, and haunting world.

If Dreiser was limited by a simple-mindedness of outlook and devoid of the remotest sensitivity to verbal effects, Sherwood Anderson could surpass him in the ultimate of limitations. Anderson's whole life was a floundering, for neither as a man nor as an artist, as he frequently confessed, could he ever make up his mind what it was that he wanted. While Dreiser, like a person engaged in pushing a rhinoceros into a phone booth, somehow incredibly approached a degree of success in his endeavor, Anderson was a man stripped of all aims except for longing and deflection. His accomplishment, if that it can be called, was in the struggle of a baffled and inarticulate man to find something to say about all the ineffable torments and yearnings that possessed him. When this was his proclaimed theme, as it is in a number of his stories, he made his only estimable statements. Anderson had a vision of the frustrations and longings of the simple and the dispossessed, but to a later generation it seemed, in its wispiness and endless questioning, rather the vision of a sleepwalker than of an artist.

The most ambitious workman of the period, Sinclair Lewis, summoned up, in a cycle of novels, a vision of American life unmatched in its variety of themes and characters. With the energy of a Zola, Lewis descended upon the small towns, the businessmen, on science, the ministry, education, politics, hotel management, feminism, Fascism, Communism, like an assured marksman picking off his enemies one by one. His weapon was satire, and through a fantastic exaggeration of the banalities of small talk he created a parody of realism that mocked the provincialism and narrowness and intolerance that were his special targets. While Lewis pursued his quarries through fiction, Henry Louis Mencken went after the same game as an essayist and critic. Both men were convinced that American society was politically corrupt, morally hypocritical, and in general a desert of mediocrity and idiocy. It was a climate in which Mencken basked with a limitless satisfaction and delight. Beginning as a Nietzschean individualist, Mencken became a sort of muckraker of the Right, lashing out with equal vigor at gentility, prohibition, censorship, bigotry, academicism, prudery, and whatever else seemed to require the touch of his truncheon. Mencken's goal was laughter and exposure; he was quite without remedies except for the remedy of being H. L. Mencken or a disciple of Mencken— a member of an *elite* who regarded life as a ridiculous joke to be enjoyed to the utmost. That it was a satire without heart became clear to the disciples of his liberation only slowly; with the Depression and the replacement among the intelligentsia of Mencken by Marx, his approval of slavery, war, and political reaction made certain his decline. Mencken's reputation today rests largely on his scholarship—on his life-long work, *The American Language.*

Mencken's influence in the twenties, however, cannot be overestimated. Not only was he indefatigable as a gadfly, but also as a press agent who promoted such talents as Dreiser and Lewis. Two of his other major enthusiasms were James Branch Cabell, author of *Jurgen* and a score of novels that contrast the tediousness of existence with the solaces of escape into a romantic dreamworld; and Joseph Hergesheimer, whose elegant and decorative novels, though not inferior to Cabell's, are little heard of today.

Never had there been so many writers heralded as "significant." Never, indeed, had there been so many writers. And never had there been such machinery of publicity and aggrandizement to serve them. The era of the bestseller and the book clubs was firmly entrenched as Elinor Wylie upheld the tradition of elegance and fragility, Carl Van Vechten took over the field of urbanity and sophistication, and Ben Hecht assumed bizarre attitudes of cynicism and violence. Ring Lardner, with a sharper ear than Sinclair Lewis's and with a sense of scorn and disenchantment Lewis never reached, impaled an assortment of middle-class figures upon a well-sharpened spear. Playwrights like Eugene O'Neill, George Kelly, Sidney Howard brought fresh material and viewpoints to the theater. Willa Cather went back to the theme of the defeat of the pioneer to create a more substantial and enduring kind of novel. Booth Tarkington, Ruth Suckow, Josephine Herbst, Ellen Glasgow, Dorothy Canfield explored the life of the middle class. It was during this period, too, that Negro writers, for the first time, were widely published and finding readers, although there had been such forerunners as Paul Laurence Dunbar; among the best known today are James Weldon Johnson, Langston Hughes, Richard Wright, Countee Cullen, and Claude McKay.

As early as 1912, a whole new school of poetry had begun

to make its appearance. Robinson Jeffers, Vachel Lindsay, Amy Lowell, Sara Teasdale, Ezra Pound, Edna St. Vincent Millay published their early work. Two Middlewesterners, Carl Sandburg, later to become the most formidable of Abraham Lincoln's biographers, and Edgar Lee Masters, were mining American speech for a realistic and altogether native poetry previously staked out by Whitman. Edwin Arlington Robinson, who had brought out his first book in 1896 without creating a ripple of interest, began to be read, along with Robert Frost, whose first appearance pre-dated Robinson's. The founding of *Poetry: A Magazine of Verse,* by Harriet Monroe, ushered in a period of unprecedented activity in verse. If the new poets displayed a diversity of aims and techniques that make hazardous any generalizations about them as a group, on one point they were united—in a deep hostility to almost the complete body of earlier American poetry, and particularly to such classroom perennials as Bryant, Holmes, and Longfellow.

In the forefront of the attack was an American poet self-exiled in Europe. As an instigator and enthusiast of the new poetry, Ezra Pound brought an unflagging energy and imagination that erupted in a stream of manifestoes, movements, theories, programs, and magazines, as well as in a body of poems to whose example every poet of consequence who followed him owes a debt. From the beginning Pound was to insist on precision and clarity in writing, on the use of "the *exact* words, not merely decorative words." He called for new rhythms based on the language of common expression to produce poetry "that is hard and clear, never blurred or indefinite." Out of such doctrine as this came the school of Imagism, whose early ornaments included John Gould Fletcher, Amy Lowell, and H.D., and a later movement, Objectivism, numbering as its chief and most gifted practitioner Pound's friend William Carlos Williams, equally talented as both short story writer and poet.

Along with another American abroad, T. S. Eliot, Pound was engaged in discovering and reassessing the literature of the past. If American writing is today animated by a wider and more discriminating appreciation of world literature than previously, it is largely because of the work of Pound and Eliot—their fresh evaluations of classical and Oriental poetry, of Dante and his predecessors, Elizabethan and Jacobean playwrights and poets, of Baudelaire, Laforgue, Rimbaud, and Corbière. Through their criticism, Pound and Eliot were not only to widen the cultural vistas of American writers, but to set forth in their own poetry a whole new range of effects. This they accomplished through an eclectic use of fragments and styles taken from the very literature they were engaged in re-evaluating. Indeed, one of the touchstones of poetic modernism is its revelation of the modern world through the device of an infinitely sophisticated fragmentation that results in a more subtle, complex, and shifting view of the world's meaning. By far the most authoritative and influential poems of our time, Eliot's *The Waste Land* and Pound's still unfinished *Cantos,* first made use of this method, a use that is still unrivaled.

While Mencken's criticism was most widely read, and Eliot's and Pound's the most influential in a subterranean way, the critical competition had never before included such a variety of antagonists. There were the Humanists, led by Paul Elmer More and Irving Babbitt, counseling a stern classicism and hostility to modernism; Van Wyck Brooks, whose early sober and searching re-examination of American literature has given way to an emphasis on the recollection of its history; Edmund Wilson, whose vigor, intelligence, and breadth of interests have saved him from the relative obscurity of many of his critical contemporaries; Vernon Louis Parrington, widely known for his lengthy study of American literature, *Main Currents in American Thought.* In recent years a group of critics who share a concern with the close analytical study of poetry, among them Allen Tate, R. P. Blackmur, Yvor Winters, John Crowe Ransom, and Cleanth Brooks, have been influential. A list of recent critics of importance would be incomplete without mentioning at least the names of Randolph Bourne, Ludwig Lewisohn, Mark Van Doren, Joseph Wood Krutch, Newton Arvin, and Kenneth Burke.

The growing revolution in language and taste in the twentieth century not only animated such contemporary poets as

Wallace Stevens, Marianne Moore, Conrad Aiken, E. E. Cummings (whose prose books, *The Enormous Room* and *Eimi*, rank among the more brilliant products of the period), Allen Tate, John Crowe Ransom, Hart Crane, W. C. Williams, Archibald MacLeish, and still younger poets, but spread to the novelists of the post–World War I generation—Ernest Hemingway, John Dos Passos, William Faulkner, F. Scott Fitzgerald.

These four, perhaps the most celebrated members of "the lost generation" as Gertrude Stein memorably baptized them, emerged from their years of war service with a highly articulate bitterness and disillusionment that was to color everything they wrote. In general more cultivated and intense than the novelists that had just preceded them, they were also better craftsmen, post-graduates from the universities of European experimentalism. From Pound, from the influential Gertrude Stein, an American expatriate in France whose insistently repetitive and rhythmic style provided her countrymen with many an uneasy and baffled moment, Hemingway discovered how to use and discipline the monotonous patterns of American speech to create a bare and chiseled precision of statement. Exploring a wide geography of experience—his boyhood in the Middle West, a series of wars, the Spain of bullfights and cafés, the Paris of expatriates, the worlds of big-game hunters, prize-fighters, rum-runners, and gangsters—Hemingway's stories and novels are documents of violent action and chaotic uncertainties, where annihilation is everywhere and only the values of stoicism, courage, and personal integrity are meaningful.

Hemingway's *The Sun Also Rises* and *A Farewell to Arms* were instantly successful. Dos Passos, Faulkner, and Fitzgerald made their first appearances on the literary scene with personalities less fully defined and with styles still flawed and unmatured. Dos Passos's *Three Soldiers*, one of the first of many novels to express a radical criticism of the First World War, was followed by a series of related novels that dealt ambitiously with no less than twentieth-century American society as a whole. Impelled by the techniques of James Joyce's *Ulysses* (which was more discussed and celebrated than influential), as much as by the theories of such French novelists as

Jules Romains, who portrayed a civilization through the lives of individuals drawn from all social classes, Dos Passos produced his massive trilogy, *U.S.A.* Covering an enormously diversified world and the lives of hundreds of representative people, the book is interlarded with three recurrent technical devices—collages of newspaper headlines, current slang, and popular songs to give rapid summations of a period's tone and sentiment; staccato and frequently ironic sketches of the lives of representative Americans like Henry Ford and Woodrow Wilson; and passages of subjective and poetic observation that contrast with the behavioristic presentation of the characters in the main narrative. Sympathetic to the political Left (though his growing disrelish for the orthodoxies of the official Communists makes itself felt in the closing sections of the book), Dos Passos pledged his most profound allegiances to the outcasts, rebels, and dispossessed of American society, and centered his satirical sights on such figures as profiteers, opportunists, advertising men, and politicians.

While Dos Passos's commitments to broad documentation and expansion led to a lack of thickness in the lives of his characters, William Faulkner's attachments, geographically narrow, centering almost exclusively on one small county in Mississippi, have led to precisely that thickness and body and particularity of individual human experience that Dos Passos lacks. Though Faulkner's county is inconsiderable in terms of mileage, it has yielded as many satisfactions as recent American literature can offer, so densely has Faulkner populated it with his doomed and haunted characters, and so thoroughly has he explored it, to the last cabin and plantation house. For Faulkner is engaged in writing no less than a vast history of Southern experience, from the middle of the eighteenth century to the present day. Even in a period like our own, when themes of violence, confusion, and decay are obsessive and omnipresent, Faulkner has pursued such themes with a particular intensity. Yet with all his concern for mutilation, incest, rape, insanity, extremes of pain, and violent death—concerns so sensationally conceived in *Sanctuary*—there is much love and pity in Faulkner, and a sense of humor not unlike that of Mark Twain. His lack of a wide audience is more likely due, not to his material, but to his lack of conventional continuity, and to a rhetoric that is often overblown and frequently meaningless.

Scott Fitzgerald, who died in 1941, had a leaner talent but a more novelistic one. Like Hemingway, he was to become a legendary and symbolic figure; while the author of *Men without Women* summed up the world of Byronic adventure, Paris in the twenties, the tough-tender literary man, Fitzgerald came to stand for the Jazz Age, wild parties on fancy Long Island estates, the middle-aged crackups of permanent collegians. Both stand for a good deal else. There is a real tragedy in Fitzgerald's career, and much that is merely trashy—the considerable hack-work he wrote for popular magazines (though not all of that is by any means contemptible)—and much that is immature. What remains most notably is *The Great Gatsby,* a definitive statement of the twenties legend—the loaded and overdecorated facade of ostentation and wealth behind which the average man's dream of superiority goes on, and *Tender Is the Night,* an equally definitive picture of the frayed-out lives and smashed careers toward which the world of the twenties pointed.

The crash of 1929 ushered in a period more notable for its meetings, manifestoes, and controversies than for its creativity. And in a world where the question of where one's next meal was coming from assumed a towering importance, this is not to be wondered at. Hundreds of writers gravitated to the political Left, dominated by the Communist party. Its rigid formulas for writing had a withering effect that can still be felt. Probably the most durable talents to develop during the period were James T. Farrell, whose trilogy, *Studs Lonigan,* carried on the Dreiser tradition; Kenneth Fearing, whose trenchantly satirical poems of urban life seemed a last extreme gasp of protest against Whitmanian optimism; and Nathanael West, a satirical novelist of uncommon originality. Thomas Wolfe established himself with a series of defiantly autobiographical novels, and Erskine Caldwell emerged with his studies of depravity and fantastic behavior among the back roads of the South.

The post-Depression years were notable for an atmosphere

of creative debility; fewer new writers of originality appeared; and only a handful of the older writers, most of them poets, seemed able to push ahead to maturity. Those who were sensitive to the lineaments of dead ends and turning-points could detect, in a growing nostalgia for the 1920s, a symptom of the times. This nostalgia, far from confining itself to the recent past, reached back even further, and one of the major publishing phenomena of recent years has been literary revivalism on a major scale. Henry James, Melville, Hawthorne, Scott Fitzgerald are only a few of the writers who have been rescued, in these cases, from obscurity, the classroom, or misinterpretation. It is probably not by chance that many of the novelists who figured in this revival were men preoccupied with form, for it was precisely a lack of this preoccupation, indeed an indifference or imperviousness to the problem of form, that had characterized so much of recent American fiction. There were some notable exceptions—in the stories of Katherine Anne Porter and some of her younger feminine disciples, in Allen Tate's novel, *The Fathers,* in Djuna Barnes's *Nightwood,* in Hemingway's earlier books, in Glenway Wescott, Willa Cather, Thornton Wilder, John O'Hara.

It was to the example of Henry James that a good many of these novelists aspired. And it was James, more than any other figure in American literature, who represented a significant break in its history. His expatriation, his profound and inflexible concept of the task of the writer, his mastery of form, his skepticism and irony, his international attitude, his highly conscious use of the methods of such Europeans as Flaubert, Balzac, and Turgenev, all combined to set him apart from the men of letters who had preceded him. It is possible that his revival, along with that of Melville, Hawthorne, Henry Adams, and a number of other earlier writers, is as significant as any literary activities of the last few years.

III

"Art Is Not a Weapon,"
1946–50

Byron Browne

Among the American painters working in an international style—and their number has grown enormously in recent years—Byron Browne has been one of the handful whose work has taken on new dimensions with each of his successive exhibitions. Browne has marked himself off from those artists of the fixed idea—*their* number has always been enormous—who stake out claims on molehill-sized areas and plow until well after numerous sour harvests are in. He is a painter who moves on restlessly to problem after problem. One might complain that Browne's prodigality could at times do with a brake: I have seen several canvases of his that another less squandering artist could stretch out into a fertile and protracted "period."

But Browne is far from ready to move on to any location, and, importantly, along with him he drags the best of his past. This luggage includes a continuing devotion to nature and the human image, his admiration for the Venetians and for primitive art, and the equipment of one of the most crafty and brilliant colorists we have. It includes, perhaps most notably of all, a delight in the physical qualities of paint and textures that has never been more arresting than in these new canvases. Scratched, glazed, sanded, scumbled, their surfaces are marked by a grainy, sensuous, heroic character that match and advance Browne's larger conceptions.

"You can tell immediately," Manny Farber has written,

From the announcement for an exhibition of Byron Browne's paintings held in November, 1946, at the Samuel M. Kootz Gallery in New York.

"from the way the surface is worked just how pleasurable painting is to the artist, how thoroughly he has painted himself out, how hard was his problem." On the basis of this, Browne's gratification must be immense; but this is something at which I can only guess. I have no need at all to guess about my own admiration for most of these vital, packed, and robust paintings.

Robert Motherwell

Painting should be music. Painting should be literature. Painting should be propaganda, an anecdote or an arrow pointing to a path of salvation. Painting should be a vertical or horizontal window that opens on a world of ladies with parasols and appealing children, cows in gently flowing streams, a bunch of flowers, or a bowl of fruit good enough to eat. These were, on various occasions, the beliefs of the past. They are also the beliefs of your Aunt Cora, the people next door, half Fifty-seventh Street, and Mr. Truman.

The beliefs to which the most advanced painters of our own time give their allegiance were foreshadowed by Flaubert, who, interrupting himself from his torments with the world-haunted manuscript of Madame Bovary, parted company with his own century to set down this unfulfilled desire: "What I should like to write is a book about nothing at all, a book which would exist by virtue of the mere internal strength of its style, as the earth holds itself unsupported in the air. . . ."

"A book which would exist by virtue of the mere internal strength of its style. . . ." This is the literary equivalent of the canvases of Robert Motherwell. He has pushed the major emphasis of abstract painting to one kind of Ultima Thule. The Cubists, even while engaged in breaking down subject matter, still clung to it, with however slippery a grasp, and the masterpieces of Cubism proclaim the entrance of a new concept of space while paying a mocking but not unaffectionate tribute to a limited, enclosed world of bottles, guitars, wine-

Magazine of Art, March, 1948.

glasses, newspaper headlines, playing cards, sliced lemons, and the human figure. Even in their collages—which may have originated in the spectacle of the peeling hoardings of Paris—collages in which paper and paint are arranged lovingly for their own sakes, this subject matter persists.

In Motherwell, however, a new kind of subject matter becomes manifest. It is paint itself. The paintings are quite simply "about" paint. Fathered, curiously enough, in view of his most recent work, by Mondrian and continuously nourished by Picasso, from whom Motherwell "lifts" objects and passages with complete acknowledgment (and in a manner far more likable and disarming than do those painters who are merely under the influence of some particular period of the Spaniard). Motherwell assumes the full consequences of the furthest tendency of abstract art. His circular forms are not oranges or abstractions of oranges, heads or abstractions of heads; his rectangles, blots, blurs, and brushstrokes assert nothing but their own existence, their own identity and individuality. They are objects from their own world, and that world is the world of paint. Motherwell's insistence upon this concentration and definition is as fierce as Céline's insistence of hell on earth or the insistence of the air on its own transparency.

Motherwell's achievements in collage are well known. It is dogma in certain advanced quarters to speak with disfavor of collage—in Paris, where John Steinbeck is admired, they are reportedly bored by it—and Motherwell perhaps has been infected a bit by these views. The vicissitudes of taste, of fashion, play major roles in the world's comedy; it was not so long ago that the Dadaists, who conceived of collage as a refuse heap, were using it as a device aimed at the annihilation of painting. They were serious if unsuccessful except for their nuisance value. Since the collages of Picasso, few artists have attempted the medium until recently, and some, like Dove, turned collage into something charming and sentimental; if there were avant-garde valentines, one would have to look no further. Motherwell, picking it up where it had been dropped in the twenties by Picasso, refurbished it with his own personality and highly charged color sense, with fresh surfaces and materials, to produce works of great spontaneity and power. They easily rank with his paintings.

"I begin painting with a series of mistakes," Motherwell has written with candor of a sort usually unflaunted by artists. "My pictures have layers of mistakes buried in them—an X ray would disclose crimes—layers of consciousness, of willing." Here is a clue to the sources of the unique in Motherwell, to the quality that encloses him in his own particular glass case. It is division, that schism in the mind that comprises so much of our modernity, a rupture from whose conflicts we may make art or by which we may be destroyed. In Motherwell, these conflicts define themselves as a declared, full-fledged, and recognized war. On one side are ranged recklessness, savagery, chance-taking, the accidental, "quickened subjectivity," painting, in the words of Miró, "as we make love; a total embrace, prudence thrown to the wind, nothing held back"; on the other, refinement, discrimination, calculation, taste—how Motherwell avoided French blood and birthplace is a puzzling question—"layers of consciousness, of willing." It is out of the continual encounters and contests of these opposites that his paintings, marked everywhere on their surfaces with signs of battle, emerge.

Miró and Modern Art

Miró is, in a sense, the first Imagist in modern painting. The Imagists fixed on exactitude, precision, bareness of statement as methods for dealing with a carefully defined and controlled subject matter that would result in "signs of something" (Miró's term). Miró has arrived at painterly equivalents that permit him to create works which, in their purity and immediacy, never go beyond themselves, that adhere, like a successful Imagist poem, to the business at hand. The separated, scattered, and alienated objects that inhabit his canvases—men, women, moons, and stars—are a series of subimages grouped to form a brilliant major image. Until Miró, no other painter worked in quite this way. Picasso is continually referring to models, rooms, architecture, events, particular identities. Matisse is similarly tied down to the specific interior, the specific figure, however freely he may deal with them. Klee sometimes approached the method, but in Klee there is a not infrequent suggestion, present or lurking, of the symbolization of the whimsical, the pathetic, or the ineffable, and the continual suggestion that the title of a work will add something, not only to one's understanding of the painting, but to the painting itself. On the other hand, most of Miró's titles are, except to the most aggressively dense museum directors, superfluous. All Miró's work of recent years deals with the refinements and regroupings of a carefully selected stock company of images, intensified until the painting and the poetry are inseparable. They do not lend themselves to

Review of *Joan Miró* by Clement Greenberg, *Partisan Review* 16 (March, 1949).

the making of large statements. They are merely, at their best, perfect. This method was slow in evolving, and Clement Greenberg has put together an excellent book, beautifully presented and containing over one hundred reproductions, with six color plates, tracing its beginnings and developments. Not only does this volume sum up the shockingly scant literature on Miró, but it provides a full-dress occasion for the operation of Greenberg's analysis, which heretofore has not been put to work on an individual painter in so detailed and extended a manner. Freed from the commitments that accompany the reviewing of reputations unfixed, Greenberg writes here with greater persuasion and density, and with what one might have predicted in advance—an absence of those mixed reproofs, shiftings, and assured pinnings of blue ribbons that must necessarily, I suppose, mark the work of the only American critic regularly, seriously, and ambitiously engaged in evaluating contemporary painting.

I can only suggest briefly the range of Mr. Greenberg's concerns: a detailed account of the influence on Miró of his early teachers, of Fauvism, *Art Nouveau,* Cubism, Surrealism, and his native Catalonian art; Miró's relationship to hedonism and the grotesque; the role of France, along with internationalizing artists of every country, in nourishing such artists as the Spaniards Picasso and Miró. (Sometime it might be a good idea to reverse the roles, emphasizing what the Spaniards and other non-French artists brought to the international style, and assess what is left.) There are penetrating, but for my liking, overbrief, analyses of Miró's successive manners and of numerous individual paintings.

Greenberg is in general so good on Miró's painting that his remarks on Miró himself seem gratuitous and ill-considered. He refers, near the end of his essay, to the artist on the occasion of his visit to New York in 1947. "Those who had the opportunity to meet Miró while he was here," writes Greenberg, "saw a short, compact, rather dapper man in a dark blue business suit. . . . He is slightly nervous and at the same time impersonal in the company of strangers, and his conversation and manner are non-committal to an extreme. One asked oneself what could have brought this bourgeois to modern painting, the Left Bank, and Surrealism." Others who had the opportunity to meet Miró saw a man equally short, compact, rather dapper, and with a distinctive military bearing, who wore a pin-stripe suit, a violet shirt, a brilliant red and green tie of South American origin with lines that suggested those of his own paintings, and an expensive pair of pointed cinnamon-colored shoes of soft suede. I found him not "slightly nervous" at all, but extraordinarily so, and markedly non-bourgeois in his social behavior. He struck me as lonely, socially uncertain, and so intensively and exclusively an artist that only in painting is he able to find a genuine existence—one to whom the conventional demands of social life are of the slightest concern. Indeed, on more than one occasion during his New York visit, Miró's silence and indifference provided some genuine and bona-fide bourgeois, who are by more than anything repelled by those who refuse to communicate or *fit in,* with moments of real discomfort. The issue suggests the remarks of Valéry on La Fontaine:

> Who could be more misleading than those truthful men who confine themselves to telling what they saw, as if we had seen it ourselves. . . . One of the most serious and logical men I ever knew generally appeared to be the soul of levity; a second nature clothed him with nonsense. And our minds are like our bodies in this respect: whatever they feel to be most important, they wrap in mystery and hide from themselves; they distinguish and defend it by placing it at a depth.

This rather interpolated concern of Greenberg's with Miró's personality seems to me the one serious flaw in a monograph that is otherwise, both in its text and choice of reproductions, one of the best summaries of a modern artist of which I know.

Weber and Hofmann

A circumstance of publication dates has brought about, in these books, the uneasy confrontation of two American painters, both of them men nearing the age of seventy, and each, in his own way, a significant and unusual figure in present-day painting. But aside from the matter of patriarchal kinship, and a shared capacity for personal enthusiasm, Max Weber and Hans Hofmann could scarcely be more dissimilar. A meeting of David Rose and Stravinsky—though this is possibly a bit unfair to at least one of the men concerned— roughly suggests the approximate atmosphere of dissonance.

Max Weber, the subject of Lloyd Goodrich's monograph, has played one of the most singular roles in American art, having made his debut shortly after the turn of the century as a unique if somewhat unreliable New York advance agent for the most extreme modes then current in Paris. Exposed at first hand to the beginnings of Cubism and to the teachings of Matisse during his years abroad, from 1905 to 1909, Weber returned to the United States to give this country its first taste, however diluted and vanilla-flavored, of European modernism. Of its kind, as Mr. Goodrich correctly points out, Weber's was "the most advanced experimental painting being produced in America in these years." Saturated in Fauvism and in the work of Picasso, but unmarked by efforts to coordinate, resolve, or extend the two (one 1910 painting, for instance, is Matisse almost brushstroke for brushstroke; another, from the same year, is an inferior echo of the figures in *Les Demoi-*

Review of *Max Weber* by Lloyd Goodrich and *Search for the Real* by Hans Hofmann, *Partisan Review* 16 (May, 1949).

selles d'Avignon), his exhibited productions thus antedated by several years the fireworks of the Armory Show and the revelation of the body of work responsible for Weber's own.

Since that time, Weber has pursued a remarkably steady course of fidelity to the School of Paris as he found it forty years ago—conventionalizing and stiffening Cézanne (Weber's figures in these canvases often seem to be supported from behind like cardboard cutouts used in drugstore displays); importing Futurism, in somewhat the manner of Stella, for accounts of metropolitan dynamism; mixing, during the Depression, a coarse "social content" with Cézannism; and, in recent years, working up a more independent and lyrical freedom of line which has operated largely on Hebraic themes of a pronounced sentimentality. But where Weber's early canvases resemble inferior and off-register reproductions of their French originals, the recent ones, however strident their claims to the spontaneous, are merely thin and embarrassing *caricatures* of Cubism. It is not surprising that Weber is considered so mouth-watering a figure by the art schools and by such institutions as the Whitney Museum of American Art.

If Weber's career has been a coasting on a plateau, that of Hans Hofmann resembles a slow uphill walk, climaxed by a spectacular spurt to the finish line. Born in Bavaria and subject to the same exhilarating force in Paris that animated Weber, Hofmann moved ponderously, experimenting and studying for years in his search for a highly personal way of seeing—a search well documented by this volume that Miss Weeks and Mr. Hayes have edited. Although Hofmann went through many of the same stages of influence as Weber, these were not permitted to become occasions for submission or stasis. For over twenty years, Hofmann did not exhibit at all; but his ideas, given shape through his long career as a teacher both in Europe and, since 1930, in this country, have probably had more concrete, valuable, and ascertainable results than those of any other figure of the period. There are, for instance, almost no painters of merit among those responsible for the current renascence in abstract work here—a renascence beside which our recent literary activity seems doubly wan and disheartening—who are not marked in some way by

Hofmann's example; and the indebtedness of several of them is heavy indeed. Hofmann's importance lies in his unremitting insistence on the seriousness and self-sufficiency of plastic expression and in his insight into the nature of abstract order—insight that has never become hardened into blocks of modernist orthodoxy. The examples of his teaching and ideas are too often employed, mistakenly, I think, as truncheons with which to club his paintings. There is little point in assigning him a numerical rank in a list of the best painters now working, nor does the quality of his work require any defense from me. I merely find it wonderful—a word that still has some freshness because it is not often one can use it these days—to see a man of Hofmann's years producing, with such passion and joy and inventiveness, his finest canvases. One thinks of Yeats, and Schweitzer.

Dondero and Dada

Since early in March a congressman named George A. Dondero, from the *Chicago Tribune* section of Michigan, has been sounding off in the House of Representatives from time to time on the subject of modern art. Like Hitler, Sir Alfred Munnings, R. A., Winston Churchill, and Stalin's art critic Kemenev, who calls modern art "hideous and revolting," Mr. Dondero is a most vocal and impassioned enemy of modernism. "Human art termites" in this country, it seems, are "boring industriously to destroy the high standards and priceless traditions of academic art." Subversive elements are at work throughout the art world—among the critics of all the New York papers and art magazines, in the Museum of Modern Art, the Art Institute of Chicago, the Fogg Museum, and even on the board of judges of the Hallmark Christmas Card Company. Things have reached a stage where "most of the finest artists that our nation numbers no longer exhibit at all." (It would be interesting to have the names of these manacled creators, but Mr. Dondero keeps a dignified silence as to their identity.)

Although the congressman has admitted he seldom visits an art gallery or museum, he has picked up a fairly wide range of aversions. In a warming spread-eagle manner that any servant of the people might envy, he calls "the roll of infamy without claim that [his] list is all-inclusive: dadaism, futurism, constructionism, suprematism, cubism, expressionism, surrealism, and abstractionism. All these isms are of foreign origin and truly should have no place in American art."

The Nation, November 5, 1949. Reprinted by permission.

Now Mr. Dondero is something of a Dadaist himself; and though his performance thus far does not quite rank him a place with, say, either Tristan Tzara or the Ritz brothers, he is improving as he goes along. Indeed, Dondero's most recent performance, late this summer, is far and away his most impressive. Currently there are at least four highly esteemed methods of attacking modern painters: (a) they are insane; (b) they "cannot draw" (cherubs, picturesque old houses, pigs killing reptiles, pretty girls, etc.); (c) they are engaged in a sinister conspiracy to make the bourgeoisie nervous and unsure of themselves; (d) they are Communist propagandists.

On August 16 Mr. Dondero chose the last method, and charged that modern art is—lock, stock, and barrel—a weapon of the Kremlin. The fact that the nationalist academicism he approves is also the official and only permissible art under the Stalinist dictatorship does not appear to trouble him at all—a Dadaist maneuver of the highest order. To add to the comic spirit of the affair, Stalin's American followers, the most devotedly solemn Dadaists of our time, have been busy with manifestoes protesting against the congressman's line, even though many of the artists he attacks—Kandinsky, Braque, Duchamp, Ernst, Miró, Seligmann, Dalí—are precisely those branded in Russia as "bourgeois formalists" and "degenerate lackeys of a dying capitalism."

While there is a school of thought which believes Dondero should not be mentioned by name, since he is motivated, it is said, solely by a desire for publicity and enjoys seeing his name in print in any context, I cannot believe that a man of his talents can be publicized too much. What the Washington spokesman for the most reactionary wing in American art circles has to say ought to have the widest possible notoriety. When Mr. Dondero refers to Thomas Craven as the "foremost art critic in the United States," as he does, or echoes Thomas Hart Benton's charge that "many . . . effeminate elect . . . blanket our museums of art from Maine to California," or declares that "art which does not portray our beautiful country in plain, simple terms . . . is therefore opposed to our government, and those who create and promote it are our enemies," let his remarks reach audiences as sizable as those of Arthur Godfrey and "John's Other Wife." When Mr. Dondero follows the Marxist line that art is a weapon, as he does throughout his latest attack, the metropolitan press should give his remarks the fullest space.

Look, Mr. Dondero, art is not a weapon, no matter how insistently you, the Nazis, and the Communists maintain that it is. Persons desiring to make weapons do not become artists—a very difficult, uneasy, and ambiguous proceeding—but engage instead in pamphleteering, speech-making, gunpowder manufacture, advertising, the designing of flame-throwers, and so on. The man who looks at a painting and inquires about the political opinions of the artist may be an idiot or merely tiresome; he is totally unconcerned with the nature of painting. As painters we have no concern with politics; as men we are in the midst of them. Our world entails a vast individual schizophrenia, and not to grasp this is to enter a community of dwarfs. The painter whose political opinions are fashionable or vicious is that much less a human being, though the machinery for evaluating the purity of one's political opinions, Mr. Dondero and others, has not yet been perfected. I throw out these dogmatisms and one other: works of art have been created by Populists, Whigs, Tories, Laborites, Liberals, Jacobins, Democrats, Socialists, Republicans, Anarchists, Monarchists, and men with no political opinions worth speaking of. None, whether American, French, German, English, Spanish, Swiss, African, Dutch, or of any other nationality known to me, have attempted to portray their countries in plain or simple terms. They have been engaged in tasks much more arduous, complex, and enduring.

Piet Mondrian

The work of the late Piet Mondrian, an excellent selection of which is now on view at the Sidney Janis Gallery, has been dealt with in most quarters in lavish, bumbling, or partial ways. Like any extreme and profoundly original painter, Mondrian has invited precisely this kind of treatment. Numbers of his most admiring followers and disciples, for example, have seized on and isolated the canvases of his last years as ultimates both in the history of twentieth-century painting and in his own career; and it is these canvases that are also pointed to, with a weird mixture of pride and slightly sooty purism, as those that have created so unmistakable a dent in contemporary design, architecture, printing, interiors, linoleum, and so on. But this is a curious way of complimenting an artist.

The Janis show, much to its credit, releases the Dutch painter from this aesthetic type-casting by a rigorous and fresh attention to all phases of his career. Small though it is, it gives a clearer and wider notion of his work as a whole than did, I should say, the Museum of Modern Art's much larger Mondrian show in 1945. A majority of the twenty-nine paintings here have never before been shown in this country. Some of them are of considerable interest, not only on their own terms, but because they fail to confirm the currently fashionable notion that Mondrian's career was a succession of me-

The Nation, November 5, 1949. Reprinted by permission. With this article Kees succeeded Clement Greenberg as art critic for the *Nation.*

thodically calculated upward steps—something along the line of nineteenth-century progress at its rosiest.

Particularly in the 1912 and 1913 Cubist canvases—painted before his association with the de Stijl movement and his elimination of all curved lines from his work—in which wonderfully varied grays and Mars yellows alternate, there are a fluidity and pulsation that have more in common with our nervous contemporary sensibility than the last canvases, however notable their successes, where "purity," the wall-like white ground, architectural concepts, flatly applied pigment of primary color, and ruler-edged bars of black have indeed succeeded in reaching "the logical consequences" of the Cubists' discoveries. Or have they? There are also "logical consequences," a variety of them, in the 1914–17 paintings—small black rectangles and modified cross-shapes scattered across a white or yellow ground—and in the "Composition 1914," with its arrangement of pastel cobblestone forms centered in a clearing mist. If there is a single impression to be carried away from the exhibition, it is the qualitative uniformity of a career ordinarily defined as largely significant for Mondrian's "major step," when he began his fierce concentration on the crossing of verticals and horizontals.

It should be late enough by now, in view of the diverse works that have developed from Cubism, to question the entire imperativeness of the "logical consequences" line. There are as many "logical consequences," it can be seen, as there are sensibilities to deal with them; and there are methods as well that have little or nothing to do with "logic." Is a straight line more "logical" than a curved one? Works of art will continue, no doubt, to emerge from both "logical" and "illogical" attitudes, along with others that escape such channelings.

Meanwhile, Mondrian's influence has been, on the whole, more restrictive than liberating. It has produced a vocal group of disciples and imitators, but scarcely any who have gone on to something more than, in a sense, the anonymous. Once one accepts the idea, as the complete Mondrian follower has done, with a Calvinistic spirit rare among painters, that "the solution of Mondrian is the last accomplishment in the development of Western painting," only a vista of replicas and approximations emerges. Like Gertrude Stein's, Mondrian's effect—and I refer to the effect of his late work, not the work as a whole—points toward the hypnotic; his followers have glimpsed a mold rather than a suggestion. Hence their hostility to nature in any but the most limited sense, to the use of forms that signify or relate to anything but themselves, their lack of interest in texture and paint quality—Scotch tape, in Mondrian's "Victory Boogie Woogie," served his purposes in some ways better than pigment—and, in their own work, a general sense of refrigeration. Mondrian, in his writings, is not too clear along these lines. "We come to see," he wrote, "that the principal problem in plastic art is not to avoid the representation of objects but to be as objective as possible." But the direction of most of the vital and original abstract work in recent years has moved away from Mondrian's views toward the exact opposite—toward the subjective and autonomous. From the ramparts of these opposing attitudes, two sizable armies of contemporary painters look out at each other with a marked lack of sympathy. The best of Mondrian, in this atmosphere, seems an accomplishment rather at a distance.

Alfred Maurer; Alexander Calder; "What They Said"

The Whitney Museum is showing a large retrospective of the late Alfred Maurer's work, now buttressed by a smaller show of his at Bertha Schaefer; and quite aside from the associations of Maurer's unhappy life, his neglect by the public, and his suicide, there is a profound sadness in the painting of this talented and sensitive American artist. If talent and sensitivity, plus an intent awareness of European modes, were sufficient to nurture a career, Maurer would have found himself as well equipped as any painter of his time. Breaking with academic and salon painting and a well-cleared road to conventional success—a jury that numbered Eakins and Homer among its members gave him the Carnegie gold medal in 1901—Maurer abandoned at an early stage his Whistler-inspired ladies and genre studies for the dangerous pathways of Impressionism, Fauvism, Cubism, and the abstract. Along with Max Weber, whose directions he shared without the burden of Weber's coarseness and sentimentality, Maurer can fairly be called the most advanced American painter of his time. Yet how dated and fragile, fragmentary, and tentative are the majority of his paintings, how soaked with the nostalgia of assumed styles that no longer move us except through their originators. It required a degree of assertiveness and strength to limber up the strait-jacket of Paris that next to none of the American painters of Maurer's time could sum-

The Nation, December 10, 1949. Reprinted by permission.

mon. Only a few men, such as Marin and Demuth, possessed the centrality of purpose, the personal obsession, that spared them the fate of playing endless variations from a score composed by those whose dominance and control were largely overpowering. Considering the frustrations of his life, the lack of acclaim, the many buried and bitter years, it is a double triumph that Maurer, in his best paintings, broke through, however momentarily. The doily still-lifes, especially, are unforgettable canvases.

At a time when many sculptors are tending their statements, Alexander Calder, at Buchholz, remains the most unworried and spontaneous of them all—the liberated engineer on vacation constructing for the most sophisticated playgrounds imaginable. That Sartre was moved to write of him recently is incredible; no art could be more removed from *Angst* and the self-questioning of literary men; soon, no doubt, we shall be enlivened by a piece on Dufy by Dean Inge. Among the seventeen mobiles of Calder's on view, color seems at times applied somewhat arbitrarily and often meaninglessly, but his sense of tension and balance is as resourceful as ever, particularly in the daring "More Extreme Cantilever," a seven-foot, three-legged tower that is paired off against a barely existent arrangement of wires by a long metal span, and in the pagoda-like "The Bleriot." Calder's metal objects now find themselves increasingly discovered in unexpected positions that suggest preoccupations with the human form similar to Balanchine's in choreography. Even the failures here show no sign of strain, only a guileless spontaneity out of control.

At Durand-Ruel an instructive show has been assembled on the idea of confronting a number of masterpieces of nineteenth- and twentieth-century painting with selected unflattering remarks on the artists by writers and art critics. Called "What They Said," the exhibition makes woefully clear the scarcely novel intelligence that art criticism is no more closed to the ignorant and foolish than are the fields of science, industry, law, government, medicine—or painting. And nothing, certainly, is more conducive to a warm rush of superiority and

self-congratulation than an event such as this, with ourselves—
and Delacroix, Manet, Corot, Monet, Renoir, Seurat, Van
Gogh, Cézanne, Gauguin, Picasso, Degas, Matisse, Rouault,
and Braque—triumphant, and the "critics" exposed for the
philistines and fatheads they were. (The inclusion of the re-
marks by Strindberg, Wilenski, and Clement Greenberg, how-
ever, seems merely crotchety and gratuitous.) That advanced
work in all fields of the arts is vilified and ridiculed one ac-
knowledges with varying degrees of annoyance, fatalism, or
disgust; the garland of dispraise that forms the exhibition's
catalogue necessarily gives no indication that it is in any way
representative of the total criticism these artists received,
though it is, God knows, common enough. As a little anthology
of misjudgment, prejudice, and *arrière-garde* stupidity, it is,
however, a gold mine. Valensol in *Le Petit Parisien* (1904) on
Cézanne: "The procedure somewhat recalls the designs that
school children make by squeezing the heads of flies between
the folds of a sheet of paper." (The French, celebrated for their
encouragement of the arts, are, curiously, outstanding at this
sort of thing.) Roger Ballu (*Inspecteur des Beaux Arts*, 1877):
"One must have seen the canvases of Cézanne and Monet to
imagine what they are. They provoke laughter and are lamen-
table. They indicate the most profound ignorance of drawing,
of composition, and of color." Royal Cortissoz, who, along with
Thomas Craven, is a particularly rich source of hatchet work
on anyone more advanced than Louis David, delivered this
judgment: "Post-impressionism as a movement, as a ponder-
able theory, is . . . an illusion." Frank Jewett Mather, Jr., in the
Nation (1913): "The more perverse expressions of Matisse's
mode as expressed in the bulbous nudes, empty schematic
decoration, and blatantly inept still-life will merely reinforce a
first impression, based on their work that is relatively nor-
mal . . . it is essentially epileptic." Maurice de Vaines (1847) on
Corot: "This black and mangled mass, would that be a tree?
This gray slab, would that be called water? And should one
sense a sky in this muddy, flattened obscurity of violet-colored
dragging strokes? M. Corot does not know . . . how to see and
paint."

Whether artists are any better served today—on the one hand by those critics who carry on in the tradition of the above, or on the other by the much more commonly encountered variety who merely describe, are tolerant to the point of vapidity, passionless and uncommitted—is another question.

"The Atmosphere in Art Circles Seems Increasingly Grayer"; Adolph Gottlieb

The atmosphere in art circles, here in New York at least, seems increasingly grayer, a good deal emptier than in years, and charged with stasis. One would set this down with more hesitation had not the grayness taken on such body and richness of late, and did not so many people in a position to know speak of it and let it influence their action. The torpor and despondency that have pervaded literary circles for some time seem to have widened their area of saturation.

Yet more than a few painters continue to produce at a higher level than the "cultural situation" apparently provides for. The demand for their work is infinitesimal. A hypothetical gallery that depended solely on the sales of the works of the nine or ten best-known advanced painters would do well to show the profits of a neighborhood candy store. One of the most important, celebrated, and influential painters in the country had for years found it impossible to market his work; the situation of even such a hard-pressed and badgered forerunner as Pissarro, for instance, seems enviable by comparison. One sale a year, to many painters, is a refreshing novelty. In a sense it is difficult not to agree with Herbert Read's assertion that cabinet painting has lost all economic and social justification. Such a point of view will, of course, be meaningless to those who snap up the works of such facile academic fabricators as Walter Stuempfig, whose "glowing

The Nation, January 7, 1950. Reprinted by permission.

light" and aged-in-the-wood literalism have brought comfort to *Life*, the art journals, and all earnest admirers of exhausted modes.

From an economic standpoint the activities of our advanced painters must be regarded as either heroic, mad, or compulsive; they have only an aesthetic justification, and even this, one feels, has become increasingly meager. Morale has dwindled; it would be hard to name a painter who is working at a high and steady level of intensity—here or in Europe—in a sense remotely approaching that of Cézanne, Van Gogh, or the Cubists early in their careers. One is continually astounded that art persists at all in the face of so much indifference, failure, and isolation. Van Gogh could write, "Now it is getting grimmer, colder, emptier, and duller around me," while still insisting that "surely there will come a change for the better." Today we are not likely to insist too strongly on the chances of so interesting a modulation. And in these times, if we were dealing with Van Gogh as a contemporary, we should handle things differently: he would be "recognized," would show annually on Fifty-seventh Street, be stroked, complimented, sell a few canvases, go to cocktail parties, and be *tamed*. Not tamed too much, however. He might even find it possible to write that "it is getting grimmer, colder, emptier, and duller . . . and things go along, worsening only a little."

If advanced painters suffer from the knowledge that their canvases, after the usual three weeks exposure to the light, are destined for a long period of dust-gathering in the racks of a gallery or in their own studios, they can take little more comfort from the proportions of their audience. An exhibition that attracts as many persons as go to fill up a movie house for one performance is successful in the extreme. Such gallery-goers will consist almost exclusively of other painters, collectors (most of whom are not collecting at the moment), art critics, students, art instructors, and museum officials, dealers from other galleries, relatives, and friends. Unable to gain a living from what he is most capable of doing, the contemporary American painter, like the poet, turns to the classroom. Today more painters than ever are teaching, for our society is fantastically devoted to the idea that the young be instructed and that still more painters be encouraged so that any valid work they produce may be ignored more completely. From the foundations responsible for fellowships and grants a serious painter can expect nothing: these act as mechanisms which function marvelously in supplying blue ribbons to the second-rate; it is scarcely news that the Guggenheim Foundation in particular has shown unerring skill in rejecting the applications of those artists whose work most deserves aid. And so it goes.

The past decade has accounted for an unprecedented burgeoning among a new school of Abstractionists, whose originality and seriousness exist in their own terms—and in truly *international* terms—rather than as a minor branch of the School of Paris. We may be, as James Thrall Soby has pointed out, "at the beginning of an era in which the artists of the Western world will try to communicate from country to country instead of through the Parisian switchboard." Meanwhile the problem of communication of a much more modest, immediate, and local variety remains overwhelming.

In this atmosphere it is heartening to note the development and modifications in the work of Adolph Gottlieb, at the Kootz Gallery. Gottlieb's reputation has thus far rested on the steady production of pictographs—diversified rectangles enclosing hieroglyphic forms—notable for their diversity and sense of the mysterious. Though many of the canvases in his new show retain this formula without strain or exhaustion— to some extent through a shift to a more airy and paler range of color than he has used before—the most striking canvases are those in which his forms have broken loose from their pictographic enclosures to declare a new sense of independence and motion. Outstanding, too, is a stunning isolated canvas of a single totemistic figure of black sand—a figure that seems the sum of a pictograph's parts. This willingness to change and experiment at a crucial stage of his career is perhaps the most important aspect of the most interesting show of this artist's work in some years.

William Baziotes; Fritz Bultman; Melville Price

William Baziotes, whose most recent paintings are being shown at the Kootz Gallery, is usually referred to as a hybrid among American painters—half-Abstractionist, half-Surrealist; certainly he is one of the last full-blown romantics of a period in which such obsessive and loving personal allegiance to the fanciful and fantastic has almost disappeared. The nostalgia for romanticism, of course, is everywhere: Baziotes manages at one and the same time to express romanticism and to be wrenched by nostalgia for it. And though most of his contemporaries have deserted "tangible" and "actual" for paintings that relate only to paint and canvas, Baziotes works, apparently, in a relatively calm acceptance of the world, however private his distortions and refinements of it. It is perhaps not so astonishing that his Surrealist inclinations have kept him closer to "recognizable form" than his leanings toward the abstract. Without being in the least literary, his work is saturated with scene, situation, movement, atmosphere, weather. His shapes, which have always unashamedly called up associations with animals, rooms, the sky, the sea, have become steadily simpler, more isolated, lonely, and at rest. If they were permitted to announce but one reason for their presence, it would no doubt be, to give pleasure.

Built up in a series of thin and spotted washes, the best of Baziotes's paintings seem to create their own light, glowing in the pigment itself. The radiance has never been turned on

---

The Nation, February 4, 1950. Reprinted by permission.

151

more strikingly by this artist than in "The Mummy," a new grass-colored canvas in which a fungus-colored seal-like form contends with a sun that shares its tone, and with a small area of brilliant blue; and this is only one of a number of first-rate paintings. In some of the smaller canvases, where pigment has been applied too flatly, space seems insufficiently packed and the lights begin to dim. But what strikes one most about Baziotes at present is his remoteness from fashion and distraction; he is his own man, with the toughness, staying power, and self-sufficiency of all good artists.

Fritz Bultman's first full-fledged one-man show, at the Hugo Gallery, brings to the foreground a young American painter who at once takes a place among the more significant advanced artists in this country. A perfectionist and a slow worker, Bultman has devoted almost four years to the fourteen canvases on view, and they are sufficient evidence of both insight and patience. Concerned with massive sculptural forms and employing few colors and relatively few basic shapes, Bultman has seemingly pared away every element that does not contribute to austerity and elegance. The show would be even better if it included his "Maize Man," which was hung in the last American Abstract Artists' exhibition and was the best painting in that show. I cannot agree at all, however, with Donald Windham, who writes the catalogue note for Bultman's exhibit, in his attempt to relate these paintings to religiosity, or more particularly to Christian symbolism. "They are true to their medium and wholly satisfying for their plastic values," Windham writes, "but they are also yantras for the contemporary Occident." This desire to insist on what is far from apparent, combined with the implied discontent with painting *qua* painting, is irrelevant to Bultman's work and, indeed, limits its significance.

The most noteworthy and pervasive development in American painting in recent years has been the trend toward "decentralized" or "all-over" painting, in which all elements of the surface have meshed or melted into one another, with no one permitted to proclaim its individual importance or its separation from the total pattern. The individual shape is trapped in an enormous machine and becomes part of it.

Those who practice this method and their followers have made elaborate claims for its superiority over all past styles, though not too convincingly; and already in the brief course of its existence the school has displayed two kinds of approach—one the careful planning of effects and the other the exploitation of spontaneity and accident. Melville Price, now holding his second one-man show at the Peridot Gallery, is one of the most ambitious and important of those who adhere to the first course. Influenced to a degree by Willem de Kooning, a painter whose lack of orthodoxy and adventurous interest in form keeps him rather on the periphery of all schools, Price develops his immensely complex and thoughtfully worked-out canvases with imprisoned shapes that lock and interlock without repose or relief. There is not much painting that affords the onlooker so little rest as Price's; Matisse might be his chief villain. I am curious what the response will be to these canvases, with their calculated "ugly" color and tormented motion. In comparison, several of the leading exponents of this school seem to derive their inspiration from Viennese waltzes or Morris chairs.

Francis Picabia and Dada;
Bernard Buffet and the
"Revolt" against Picasso

There are certain individuals who are born for one particular moment or activity—the actor with his one good role, the one-poem poet, the one-novel author, the chemist who has happened upon one splendid and revered weapon or panacea, the vaudevillian with his lone routine that every circuit knows by heart. Francis Picabia, whose work is on view at the Pinacotheca, takes his place in this company with ease and authority. Picabia seems to have existed solely for the busy and enthusiastic part he played in the birth and death of Dadaism, and the end of the Dada period appears to have left him with nowhere to go and not much of anything to do.

Convinced that the world was imbecilic and absurd, the Dadaists, with Picabia as one of their founding fathers, systematized a method of ridicule with which they hoped to destroy all values and identities. Art and literature were dumped into the same wastebasket to which all other categories were consigned; but, with perfect illogicality, the Dadaists continued to cling to painting and writing as weapons against themselves. "Those who refuse to see in the Dada movement anything but a Parisian scandal characterized by violence and buffoonery," Marcel Raymond has written, "will never understand the intense moral crisis of the 1920's and the current of anarchistic individualism, the refusal to be useful, that up-

The Nation, March 11, 1950. Reprinted by permission.

set so many traditional slogans and age-old beliefs." Perhaps. But it was in other quarters altogether that the "intense moral crisis" was being not only experienced but comprehended— by talents committed not only to upsetting traditional slogans but to salvaging and creating: Proust, Mann, Eliot, Pound, Valéry, Joyce (a non-Dadaist who deeply penetrated the Dada spirit), Picasso, Braque, Miró.

Nothing has dated more than the run of Dadaist products; and nothing illustrates more effectively the irrelevance and topicality of works that owe their being alone to a "spirit of revolt." (The poetry of Eluard is another matter.) The "totally original," the last word, has a way of fading out like an imperfectly fixed snapshot. The Dadaists, to a great extent, produced period pieces, equivalents of the whatnot, the antimacassar, and the coiffures of Theda Bara. On the other hand, the early Cubist masterpieces of Braque and Picasso have taken on greater stature through the passage of time itself. Even the Dada jokes are far from mirth-provoking at this distance; they seem even weaker than the paintings. Yet Picabia was made for the period in which he could mount a doll representing a monkey on a poster and letter it "Portrait de Cézanne."

Such embarrassments come back to haunt the eighteen works of Picabia now in New York; and another declares itself in the dates of the paintings themselves. Twelve are dated from 1908 to 1917; there follows a period of over twenty blank years; the remaining canvases are dated 1949. From the time of the death of Dada, Picabia is reported to have passed through various phases as a painter and destroyed many canvases; the ones he has now permitted to be shown are thin and unassured—colored grounds with a few scattered dots, footnotes to an altogether enervated non-Objectivism. The earlier canvases, playful and now innocent indeed of fantastic machines that satirize the whole world of mechanisms, at least have a very moving and altogether period flavor. The several Cubist paintings, which show a personal if haphazard talent, bolstered by hints from both Cézanne and Duchamp, do little to alleviate the melancholy of the occasion.

The latest generation of French painters was recently repre-
sented on Fifty-seventh Street by the widely publicized twenty-
two-year-old Bernard Buffet, at Kleeman. Buffet, a leader of
the current Parisian denigration of Picasso, is here set forth in
a series of rather bare and chilly still-lifes that employ a not
unfamiliar conglomeration of props—bottles, fish, tableware,
lemons, and coffee-grinders. Rigidly placed and defined by
pencil lines, the bottles are empty, the knives and forks as
starved in appearance as the haggard and emaciated young
men of Buffet's earlier canvases, the lemons shriveled, and the
coffee-grinders cleaned out of either beans or grounds.
Buffet's colors are few, tasteful, and non-assertive; his pen-
ciled signature, however, is large enough to become more
dominant an object than one of his lemons.

The "revolt" against Picasso, which Buffet and several
other of the newer Paris painters are tireless in proclaiming to
the press, seems, considering the work of these men, to be
merely verbal, and not much more to the point than a revolt
of, say, Abbott against Costello. Most of these men, it is clear,
have sizable bills to settle with Picasso; and Buffet, certainly,
has merely tidied up the manner and subject matter of certain
canvases Picasso was doing in the early 1940s. It would seem
that the younger French painters stand in a relationship to
the Spaniard that is bound to be unpalatable: they resent his
towering reputation, and they are filled with annoyance at
their inability to make a radical break with his influence.
Hence a "revolt" that can be discerned everywhere but in
their work.

Life's "Journalistic Egg";
Franklin Watkins;
Charles Demuth;
Arshile Gorky

Rumors that *Life* was planning a spread on young American artists raised expectations, in some quarters, at least, of the laying of another massive journalistic egg. Yet surprises have, on occasion, taken place. The piece has now appeared ("Nineteen Young American Painters," issue of March 20) and amply confirms the sourest anticipations. By any standards, this is pretty stale cake. For the "best" nineteen young painters that the magazine has dredged up, by way of inquiries to "the country's museums and art schools . . . of thirty-eight states"—what about the other ten?—are surely the counterparts of nineteen other young painters *Life* might have presented ten years ago. Nothing seems to have changed. What is significant and vital in recent art activity in this country—the emergence of a radical, original, and pervasive movement animated by Abstract, Fauve, Expressionist, and Surrealistic influences, which has had its most extreme expression in the work of such enormously influential men for young artists as Hans Hofmann, Jackson Pollock, Arshile Gorky, Willem de Kooning, and Richard Pousette-Dart—is here completely bypassed. It is as if one wrote an account of recent pictorial journalism without mentioning *Life* and its contemporaries.

What *Life* serves up, in general, is a cast of art-school medal-

The Nation, April 8, 1950. Reprinted by permission.

winners and housebroken scholarship perennials whose feet are firmly planted in the past and have taken root there. Here are "social protest" paintings of both the literal and fantastic varieties, figure paintings (". . . the young Americans with a native love of natural forms behind them, have not entirely renounced the human figure," *Life* announces reassuringly), "American scene" canvases, both lyrical and grim, Braque's forms and colors watered down and poured into a landscape, an "enraged bull" out of Disney, and a number of abstractions and semi-abstractions notable for their tastefulness and timidity. "Are they signs of a new flowering of American art?" *Life* inquires. The answer is No; and the same answer will do nicely for the question: "Is *Life* seriously interested in art, whether by the young, the old, or the middle-aged?" Nineteen young artists of greater talent and adventurousness could easily have been discovered in a single county, with the application of a little knowledge or curiosity, or even the right address book, and a lot of time and money saved in writing all those museums and art schools in thirty-eight states.

The Luce publications are scarcely in a position to become New York branches of *Cahiers d'Art;* the Museum of Modern Art, on the basis of its recent offerings, seems scarcely in a position to lay proper claim to its own title. Its current show of Charles Demuth is a matter of no surprise after the museum's open-armed welcome in the past to such men as Maurice Stern, Sheeler, and Ben Shahn, and its reverence for cartloads of expendable young British and Italian painters. Indeed, Demuth is a figure of some stature beside the other artist singled out at this time for a retrospective—Franklin Watkins. The selection of Watkins may very possibly mark an all-time low in the museum's strenuous grapplings with eclecticism. What next? A Winston Churchill retrospective?

Watkins, a fiercely academic artist whose career sums up with a thoroughness of definition all that is conventional and beside the point in modern painting, is a very rare species—a man drained of style, of commitment, of obsession, who presents, in spite of his occasional gestures of melodrama, a sensibility blank and impersonal as a sheet of glass. So blank is it, indeed, that this seems less a retrospective of one man than a run-of-the-mill group show of minor American painters out of the 1920s, assembled at one of the less forward-looking university museums; even the signature "Watkins" on all the canvases fails to convince. Whether he paints an admonishing angel, a still-life, or Justice Owen J. Roberts, each manages to exude the identical degree of stiffness and consciousness of being a subject, a prop in a studio set-up. Demuth, on the other hand, was an artist of delicacy and charm whom the museum has badly served by the crowded and inclusive character of the rooms given over to him. Demuth comes off best as an illustrator: his fairly uniform low pressure, fragility, and old-maidishness were jolted more by his encounters with Zola, James, and Wedekind than by his brush with Cubism, which meant little more to him than as a superimposition. The show, unfortunately, puts too great an emphasis on his watercolors of flowers, which are repetitious and cloying in the extreme; every last daisy, fuchsia, and tuberose is made room for. Any retrospective requires selection; and Demuth demands it. Other forces prevailed on this occasion.

There is little painting of our time to match the richness, sensuousness, and elegance of the last canvases of Arshile Gorky at Kootz. Throughout his career, terminated by the artist's suicide in 1947, Gorky seemed more than ordinarily marked by a struggle to get at his own identity; yet the constant complaint was made that this artist, though a born painter if ever there was one, was pinned in a vise constructed by Miró, Picasso, and Matta. In these final canvases, Gorky worked himself through these men to declare his own being unmistakably. In a catalog note which is a model of its kind, Adolph Gottlieb refers to these canvases as "true *alla prima* painting; the ultimate in craftmanship in any period and any style." How severe a loss Gorky's death was to American painting is only now becoming clear; a forthcoming retrospective at the Whitney Museum should serve to confirm its extent. Perhaps Gorky, now that he is safely dead, will receive the recognition denied him when he was in a position to care.

Contemporary French Painting;
"Talent 1950"

Since the end of the war only a dribble of contemporary French painting has found its way to New York, and the meager examples available here have made it difficult to come up with any sweeping statement on the work of the generations trailing Picasso, Matisse, and Leger. Then, too, there has been no knowing whether the little we have been permitted to see represents average, inspired, or inferior choices. And there has been an additional difficulty in deciding to what extent the apparent slump in French art—and literature—is attributable to the extremities of the war and its aftermath. Recently we have had the very young M. Buffet, an enormous success in Paris—an experience which has not been reassuring either in regard to current French taste or to the state of "new" French painting; and we have had Dubuffet, whose work marks the only radical break with an increasingly academic and derivative abstract movement abroad. Dubuffet's singular eminence receives not even the mildest threat at Carré's current show, "Advancing French Art," which includes twenty-six canvases by six painters, two of them Russians and one a German. "Advancing" and "French" are perhaps not the most desirable terms for this occasion.

Jean Bazaine, a capable painter, is represented by work that does not show him at his best. Maurice Estève "seeks a harmony of the whole," says the catalogue note; on the basis

The Nation, May 6, 1950. Reprinted by permission.

of these works a continued search would seem to be in order. Hans Hartung's painting, possibly a result of his disastrous experiences during the war, has become more disordered and lacking in necessity. Charles Lapicque is a Ph.D. specializing in optics; his paintings look very much like the sort a Ph.D. specializing in optics might do. Nicolas de Staël and André Lanskoy, the Russians, are much freer and more open; knowing colorists, both of them obviously find great pleasure in paint. A notion exists that there is a facility peculiarly French for "finishing" a painting—the capacity for giving a canvas the final seal of completion that marks it "guaranteed genuine hand-painted oil, made in France," and many French painters do have this capacity to a marked degree. In this instance, the Russians have learned the lesson even better than the men of their adopted country; but they seem more deeply concerned with the finishing touch in a rather narrow sense (French painting in the twentieth century) than with a "contribution"—a fresh and vital approach that is felt at all stages of the painting rather than its ultimate one. Their failure is the result of adhering, not to a tradition, but to their narrow concept of what they believe constitutes this tradition. It is precisely Matisse, Vuillard, Bonnard, and Picasso (sometimes) who avoid the "finishing touch" like the plague. And it is Dubuffet who has actively mocked at it in order to go beyond a tradition that he had come to feel was, for him at least, stifling and deadening.

Last month, commenting irritably about the young American artists recently singled out by *Life*, I wrote that "nineteen young artists of greater talent and adventurousness could easily have been discovered in a single county, with the application of a little knowledge or curiosity." Working quite independently of this suggestion, Meyer Schapiro and Clement Greenberg, two of the critics most alert to serious art activity, have proceeded to assemble just such an exhibition, at the Kootz Gallery. Called "Talent 1950," it includes work by twenty-three unknown or little-known painters living in New York, most of them under the age of thirty. If it fails to reveal any breathtaking revolutionary mood or to indicate any sharp break with the course of contemporary painting,

161

the show is a notable one for a number of other reasons. It marks the first time, to my knowledge, that a show of this scope and nature has been installed in a major gallery: these are largely outcast and unrecognized painters who are ordinarily brushed off by Fifty-seventh Street. It has been chosen by men of advanced tastes, willing to take risks and make use of their own brains, instead of the ruck of cross-section fanatics and Gallup Poll characters who infest our museums and magazines. It is a very *young* show, with all such a show's uncertainties and gropings, but with enormous spirit and optimism and love of paint. This is all to the good: some of *Life*'s young painters had a middle-aged look before they got out of their twenties.

Of the artists whose work was new to me, Esteban Vicente seems easily the most accomplished—lyrical, serene, assured, soaked in culture, and, if this canvas is any indication, quite ready for a show of his own. Al Leslie's all-over canvas makes an even stronger first impression than Vicente's but it is a little too up-to-the-minute and fails to retain its original appeal after extended examination. Harry Jackson's *Triptych* takes more chances than any other painting in the show; it has great *weight;* but in asking so much Jackson has not ordered all its elements sufficiently. The best of the women—Elaine de Kooning, Clara Elkoff, Lenita Manry, Sue Mitchell, and Leatrice Rose—indicate the welcome emergence of a new school of muscular female Fauves. Manny Farber, a painter who shows far too infrequently, emerges as the strongest and most original colorist of the show, and perhaps the most ambitious painter of the lot. Hyde Solomon is inadequately represented by a small and charming watercolor; and I admired the spirit of the works by Robert Goodnough and Franz Kline.

Bradley Walker Tomlin; the "Irascibles'" Manifesto

Bradley Walker Tomlin is the most recent convert to a manner of painting for which we still have no satisfactory name—a matter of more concern as yet to the artists responsible for it than anyone else—and which is marked by a free, imaginative, and highly personal non-Objectivism that has little to do with the rigidities and orthodoxies of the official non-Objectivist ranks. In his recent show at Betty Parsons Gallery, Tomlin, who formerly worked impeccably and gracefully in the Cubist tradition, now covers his canvases with swirling calligraphy and dripping paint that become symbols of tension and discord at the same time that they act, in their totality, as achievements of order and grace. Tomlin's emotions and sense of an entire world are much more in evidence now, it strikes me, than heretofore, yet his old aloofness is still making itself felt. But we can stand, I think, a degree of aloofness, not a very common quality these days, particularly when it is as stunningly embodied as it is in such a painting as Tomlin's large *Number 20,* one of the most soundly constructed and elegant canvases to be seen this season.

One gets tired of saying, in the event of a major change in a painter's direction, that it marks an "advance" (a "great advance," an "inspired advance," a "noteworthy advance," a "bold advance," and so on), or of particularizing any one of a variety of retreats, modifications, or sidesteps; and I shall spare Tomlin the weariness of being poked into one of these

The Nation, June 3, 1950. Reprinted by permission.

always available pigeonholes. But it is dispiriting to find all the critical notices I have seen on Tomlin's show working over-time in questioning his altered manner, studded with terms such as "debatable direction" and "experimentation" that suggest heads shaken in dismay. The middle-ground critic used to have a sizable stable of tasteful middle-ground paint-ers in whose company he felt comfortable and assured; now there are not so many to provide comfort and assurance, and they are growing fewer. There is the avant-garde, and there is the great glowering world of the Academy.

For years the Metropolitan Museum has been under attack for its lack of interest in contemporary art. Its cushy Hearn fund, bequeathed to it generations ago for purchasing work by living American artists, has been left in the vaults, most of it, and what little has been touched has been spent for paint-ings that might as well have been chosen by a committee of congressmen or the ladies of the Elkhart Bide-a-Wee.

The present director of the Metropolitan, Francis Henry Taylor, makes no secret of his hostility to advanced trends in contemporary art—he reached some sort of high in philistin-ism, where competition is keen, when he compared Picasso's *Guernica* to *The Charge of the Light Brigade* and remarked that Picasso "has only substituted Gertrude Stein for Florence Nightingale." Recently, the cries of discontent at the mu-seum's policies have become louder; several influential voices have made themselves heard, among them that of James N. Rosenberg, a museum member and New York lawyer, who not long ago wrote a series of sharp and high-flavored letters which must have been embarrassing even to the elephant-hided Mr. Taylor. Whether knuckling under to such pres-sures or acting for its own mysterious reasons, the Metro-politan has suddenly become a beehive of activity directed at "recognizing" and "supporting" American art of the present. In a few weeks it promises to open an exhibition of twentieth-century paintings from its own collection—a collection hastily reinforced in the last few months by a spree of apparently frantic buying in an attempt to fill up the gaping holes so long in evidence. This show, says the museum, will "remove certain misconceptions in the critical and public mind which for one reason or another have arisen in recent years." I wonder.

In addition to its long-delayed purchasing binge, the Metropolitan has announced a jumbo national competitive exhibition, "American Painting Today—1950," to be chosen by a number of regional juries, with prizes totaling $8,500. Already, across the nation, painters' mouths are watering. The general idea suggests another proportional-representation show of the Pepsi-Cola variety; the list of the jurors—almost a solid phalanx of such academics as Jerry Bywaters, Everett Spruce, Lamar Dodd, Leon Kroll, Paul Sample, Franklin C. Watkins, etc., etc.—suggests not eclecticism or proportional representation but entrenched timidity and conservatism of the purest ray serene, it has been suggested that this jury "may surprise us" by picking an adventurous and valuable show. I look forward to this with the same warm expectations that I have of the American Legion building a series of marble shrines honoring the memory of Randolph Bourne or of Baudelaire being voted the favorite poet of the Cicero, Illinois, junior high schools. Preparations for this endeavor have been under way for "nearly a year," says the Metropolitan; it is clear that the selection of a jury as humdrum as this must easily have consumed that long a period of time.

The following letter, which I was pleased to sign, was addressed to Roland L. Redmond, president of the Metropolitan, and recently made public. It bore the signatures of eighteen painters—among them such distinguished and prominent artists as Jackson Pollock, Hans Hofmann, Adolph Gottlieb, Robert Motherwell, Willem de Kooning, William Baziotes, Ad Reinhardt, and Mark Rothko; they speak, I should guess, for a considerable number of other artists.

[We] reject the monster national exhibition to be held at the Metropolitan Museum of Art next December, and will not submit work to its jury.

The organization of the exhibition and the choice of jurors by Francis Henry Taylor and Robert Beverly Hale, the Metropolitan's Director and the Associate Curator of American Art, does not warrant any hope that a just proportion of advanced art will be included.

We draw to the attention of these gentlemen the historical fact that, for roughly a hundred years, only advanced art has made any consequential contribution to civilization.

Mr. Taylor, on more than one occasion, has publicly declared his contempt for modern painting; Mr. Hale, in accepting a jury notoriously hostile to advanced art, takes his place beside Mr. Taylor.

We believe that all the advanced artists of America will join us in our stand.

For the first time, avant-garde painters in this country have taken a united position against the Academy; this is their historical role; the Academy itself drew the lines.

IV

"As I Hurried West":
Final Installments,
1950–55

San Francisco Artists Set a Pace

Next to New York, San Francisco strikes at least this observer, after an absence of ten years, as the liveliest center of art activity in the country today. Partly because of its climate and homogeneity, the beauty of its harbor and bridges, its spectacular hills covered with white houses, suggesting a well-scrubbed Naples—and perhaps more pointedly because of the absence of anything resembling New York's gallery system. San Francisco's "artistic" atmosphere seems remarkably fluid, open, and adventurous. Young painters are serious and ambitious, but unworried, for instance, about their chances of getting a one-man show on Fifty-seventh Street.

Some of them, however, are worried about their community's responsibility to local artists. Out of this concern has come the San Francisco Art Festival, a singular undertaking for any municipality. The four-day affair, presented by the city's Art Commission, is held in the impressive Palace of Fine Arts. When it closed its doors it had clocked visitors through at the rate of two thousand an hour. Participating were more than twelve hundred painters, sculptors, and craftsmen of the Bay Area—the nine counties in and around San Francisco—in an exhibition suggesting a combination of an outdoor Washington Square show and a coexisting counterblast by the far left-wing of the advance guard, with joint general supervision by Barnum and C. B. De Mille.

Large exhibitions "representing all trends and schools" are not infrequently characterless in the extreme; but the Art

New York Times, December 31, 1950. Copyright © 1951 by The New York Times Company. Reprinted by permission.

Festival, because of its goodwill, abandon, immensity, and lack of pretentiousness in matters of standard-setting, was carried into quite another sphere—on the edge of a particularly spectacular county fair or bazaar. This, in the present instance at least, was all to the good. It is possible to grow solemn indeed about a show of twelve or fifteen paintings; but more than two thousand paintings create a reaction of an altogether different order.

The De Mille–like aspects of the festival were heightened by a setting altogether appropriate. The Palace of Fine Arts is at the edge of the approach to the Golden Gate Bridge, overlooking a lagoon swarming with active ducks, gulls, and swans. It stands somewhat precariously, for it was built only as a temporary structure for the 1915 exposition that celebrated the dedication of the Panama Canal. Reminiscent of the Paris Galerie des Machines (built in the Eiffel Tower period) and now in a state of continual disintegration, it has endured, after a fashion, for thirty-five years, serving for a time as an eighteen-court tennis center.

The state of its columns are today a cause of uneasiness, and parts of its exterior are barred to the public because of the danger from falling chunks of plaster. Semicircular, its vast armory-like interior stretches 990 feet and is 135 feet wide; it easily accommodated the ten thousand items in the fields of painting, sculpture, ceramics, textiles, printing, and architecture.

What marked the festival with a special significance was not only that the city had appropriated $10,000 to make it possible—the only city in the country spending money on any such project—but that behind its conception lay a desire to bring together and relate the whole range of the arts. Though major emphasis this year was on painting, the ultimate goal of those behind the festival is a permanent art center for annual festivals that will give more emphatic attention to music, drama, poetry, the dance, architecture, and all the crafts, as well as painting and sculpture.

The festival was enlivened by small groups of strolling musicians, recitals by modern dancers, band concerts, a showing of experimental movies, a little theater group performance of

Chekhov's "The Boor," lectures on art, and a workout by the Studio 13 Jazz Band, a vigorous Dixieland group, most of whose members are students or members of the faculty at the California School of Fine Arts.

The background of the festival's origins is not unconnected with the city's "cultural" tax, used largely in the past to support music. For the last five or six years, active pressure has been exerted on the Municipal Art Commission to use a part of this fund for the support of painting as well as music. A new organization, Artists Groups of the Bay Area, Associated [AGBAA], was founded to push the plans along. In the fall of 1946, San Francisco's first outdoor art show, officially presented by the art commission, was held in the Civic Center.

Three more shows followed, but with increasing evidence of the decorated clamshell and painted necktie schools. The local branch of Artists' Equity, hoping for something better, took the lead in formulating a written plan for an art festival, and, in cooperation with AGBAA, submitted it to the Art Commission. Then followed six months of deliberation. In the forefront of the pro-festival camp were Ernest Born, a practicing architect with an enlightened interest in the arts and an energetic member of the Art Commission; Emily Lou Packard, a painter and former head of AGBAA; Martin Snipper, present director of the festival; and Frank O. Merwin, architect for several of the outdoor shows as well as the festival.

Funds were finally granted. They included more than $4,000 for prizes and a sum covering the expenses of transporting three jurors from the East—a jury that would be "representative and not reflect any one esthetic school." The jurors chosen were Katherine Kuh of the Chicago Art Institute, Bartlett H. Hayes, Jr., of the Addison Gallery, and Lloyd Goodrich of the Whitney Museum.

The festival itself conformed to the standards for the jurors and did not reflect "any one esthetic school." Along with considerable arresting work, and even more that was skilled and competent, there was the usual woeful amount of dehydrated Cubism; the usual array of work by desert, lonely wharf, and metropolitan-pathos symbolists; admirers of

General MacArthur; and oversophisticated primitives. The jurors apparently kept carefully in mind the fact that they were selecting "civic purchase prizes."

Yet the most moving and vigorous painting in the festival came from the neo-Fauve group of abstract expressionists that has mushroomed wildly here in the last few years. Given incentive to some extent by such painters as Clyfford Still and Mark Rothko, both of whom have taught at the California School of Fine Arts, the best of these painters—Edward Corbett, Hassel Smith, Philip Roeber, and George Stillman— have sensed a general direction rather than a formula. Work by any one of these men would set New York's avant-garde seismographs aquiver. Less even, but of interest, is the work of Elmer Bischoff, Jack Leon Lowe, Jorge Goya, and Budd Dixon. The collective accomplishment of this group is strong evidence that Manhattan is by no means a lone fortress of contemporary advanced painting.

Oh, Play That Thing!

Some twelve years ago, in Washington, D.C., one of the more salutary undertakings in recent musical archivism was unpretentiously set in motion. Alan Lomax, folklore expert of the Library of Congress, adjusted a microphone near a piano in the Coolidge Chamber Music Auditorium with the intention of making a record or two with a once-famous Creole singer, pianist, composer, arranger, band leader, and self-styled "originator of jazz," the late Ferdinand Joseph "Jelly Roll" Morton.

It was the period of big-band swing music, a debased and smoothed-out variant of Morton's mature ideas; Morton himself, the most creative intelligence among early New Orleans jazzmen, had come down, through a series of catastrophic events, from a life of productivity, wealth, fame, Lincoln sedans, Victor contracts, diamond sock-supporters, and custommade silk shirts, to an obscure and seedy existence as a performer in a Washington nightspot notable for recurring periods of insolvency. Beset by asthma attacks and a bad heart, with death little more than three years away, Morton still preserved the spirit of a Renaissance lord, an undimmed talent at the keyboard, and the charm of one of the most gifted— though highly unreliable—raconteurs of the time. Lomax, a discerning judge of what to put on acetate, kept the sessions going for almost two months, while Morton uninhibitedly poured out the story of his life, interspersing reminiscences

Review of *Mr. Jelly Roll* by Alan Lomax and *They All Played Ragtime* by Rudi Blesh and Harriet Janis, *The Nation*, March 24, 1951. Reprinted by permission.

with vital piano-and-vocal work on such memorable compositions as "The Animule Ball," "See See Rider," "Kansas City Stomp," "King Porter," "Creepy Feeling," "Michigan Water Blues," and "Winin' Boy." The records, later released to the public in a twelve-volume set by Circle, form a unique and fantastic mélange of autobiography, music, and altogether personal history of New Orleans jazz.

Lomax has now produced a book on this remarkable figure. *Mister Jelly Roll*, a series of notes masking as a biography, consists largely of printed approximations of Morton's recorded talk, supplemented with Lomax's own sketchy and pot-luck research. (The number of unconsulted persons who knew Morton is an army on the march.) These notes are fascinating, certainly, but in no sense the real right thing. Mr. Lomax's recently proclaimed theory that the age of the wire-recorder will result in a golden age of biography, through an upsurge of on-the-spot verbal autobiographers, rests on a notion that effective oral monologue—of which Jelly Roll Morton was a master—is equally effective when transcribed as writing. But speech and writing, regrettably—at least for Mr. Lomax—do not work at all in the same way. Morton's spoken words, stripped of their intonations, inflections, and pauses, lose a major part of their charm. The book is heavy with a vibrancy muffled and deadened, "the tinkling piano in the next apartment," the band turning the corner four blocks down the street.

Morton stands in relationship to most other jazz artists as Bartók, Schoenberg, and Stravinsky relate to the raft of thin and derivative "serious" men who thinly and derivatively follow in their wake. He was not only one of the best singers and pianists of a period when talent was prodigal but a composer and arranger of a far more impressive and original nature than any of his contemporaries—and there have been no successors. The list of his songs, rags, stomps, and blues documents a worker as prolific as Spencer Williams or Gershwin. His best records—enough to pack an Old Overholt carton—are, measure after measure, saturated with an unmatched insight, variety, and sense of construction, with maximum attention to the resources of polyphony, rhythmic complexity, and instrumental contrast. Along with Kid Ory, Louis Armstrong, and a few other men, he kept the lyrical side of jazz, in recent years so little in evidence, alive.

Writers on jazz are not infrequently of a kitschy and razzmatazz order, substituting spurious elations for sterner and more essential requirements. Mr. Lomax is on a higher plane than this; his prose is serviceable and in general avoids sounding, as such work so often sounds, as if it were written with an old discarded reed of Pee Wee Russell's on some rapidly moving object. But a first-rate study of such a life as Morton's—as rich in "material" as the lives of Cellini or Baron Corvo—would seem to call for the talents of an Enid Starkie or a Francis Steegmuller, with allegiances to writing instead of wire-recorders.

Rudi Blesh, a dedicated and industrious jazz historian, whose writings have in the past featured a Brancusi-like purity in their devotion to the New Orleans school, has now joined forces with Harriet Janis to break rockier ground than that of Mr. Lomax. *They All Played Ragtime* is a pioneering study of the infectious syncopated piano style that swept the country in the late 1890s and declined and fell in the early 1920s. Working chiefly through personal interviews with surviving ragtime composers, many of whom at times seemed as inaccessible as Judge Crater, Mr. Blesh and Mrs. Janis establish themselves as researchers of a high and tireless order. Their book's main drawback is a warty style that occasionally suggests a mound of dill burr gherkins. Yet its exhaustive working of untapped and important material is compensatory in the extreme.

Ragtime, a mixture of folksong, banjo syncopation, and complex African rhythm, is the vigorous, intricate, highly accented pianism that preceded jazz and has permanently affected "serious" Western music from Debussy to the present. In its classic phase it was a product of a handful of devoted composers, both Negro and white, who touched off a nationwide ragtime craze. The principal hotbeds of ragtime composers were mostly in the North—Sedalia, Missouri, St. Louis ("the capital"), New York, and Indianapolis; and Blesh and Mrs. Janis have done a remarkable job in isolating and distinguishing the various schools, just as they have in treating such prolix and related phenomena as honkytonk and bordello pianists, cakewalk contests, the nature of early sheet-music publication, Negro Bohemia, the Sousa and Arthur Pryor phase, the blues-spiritual-ragtime cross-currents, ragtime's critics and defenders, and the ersatz ragtime promoted by Tin Pan Alley. Most attractive of all are the sympathy and insight they bring to their accounts of the lives of such composers as Scott Joplin, James Scott, Joseph Lamb, Jelly Roll Morton, and James P. Johnson, among dozens of others, who out of their bounteous and creative spirits have given us such enduring works as "Maple Leaf Rag," "Grace and Beauty," "Sensation," "The Pearls," and "Carolina Shout."*

---

*In addition to writing about the state of jazz music, Kees gave informal lectures on the subject, notably at symposiums like Forum 49 in Provincetown during the summer of 1949, and at the Abstract Expressionists' "school," Studio 35, on Manhattan's Lower East Side in the late forties. He also lectured on jazz at the University of California at Berkeley, and on KPFA-FM in San Francisco in the early fifties. Transcripts of these talks have not survived; their spirit, however, is suggested by the following statement taken from an interview with Kees printed in the *Provincetown Advocate,* July 14, 1949:

Authentic jazz music—a completely American phenomenon—is today almost a buried music in its own country. The so-called "popular" music and mistakenly called "jazz" that comes out of the radio and jukeboxes these days, continually reach new lows of banality and emptiness. We've been all but sunk by crooners, swing bands, and devotees of the bebop school.

In the 1920s, Europeans honored the United States for Whitman, Poe, Henry Ford, our movies, and our jazz music. Since then, and particularly since the last war, Europe has had to reckon with, among other things, our science, architecture, literature, and painting. We certainly don't need, any longer, to wait around for cues from Paris on which way to jump culturally, if we ever did: but Americans might do far worse than catch up with Europe's early appreciation of New Orleans and Dixieland music. I'm not arguing for a nationalistic pride in America as the birthplace of jazz—an attitude that was dreary enough to begin with. I'm arguing for a greater degree of attention to the kind of inspired and polyphonic music Armstrong and Morton brought to its own kind of perfection.

—ED.

A Note on Climate and Culture

A beginning must be made somewhere—even in such clouded territory as the one in which my considerations exist—so let me begin by raising this question: Is the artist in the San Francisco region a different kind of creature than his counterpart in New York, Paris, Rome, or London? And if so, how did he get that way? I take it that something along this line might concern readers living in another part of the country and thus unfamiliar with the work being done here. And, having picked this question from a number of others I might as easily have raised, let me point out at once its inadequacy. To begin with, the "artist in the San Francisco region" as such is altogether too dim and ill-defined a figure for scrutiny. The region makes room for the entire range of styles and attitudes that comprise twentieth-century art multiplicity, with allegiances ranging from the tamest traditionalism to a recently evolved and extreme neo-Fauvism of a pronounced indigenous cast.

What these artists do have in common is probably the most equable climate in the entire country and the stimulation, or the chance for it, of one of the few beautiful cities left in the world. Unlike either contemporary New York or Paris, San Francisco and environs offer the possibility of at least a measure of serenity. The effect of these benisons on the arts, however, is not very readily discerned. More apparent is the presence of a vigorous and solidly entrenched craft tradition. Perhaps no other area—and in this context it extends south

From *Painting and Sculpture* by The San Francisco Art Association (Berkeley: University of California Press, 1952).

beyond Los Angeles—is so densely populated with architects, designers, ceramicists, interior decorators, landscape gardeners, and entrepreneurs of modern furniture. Their presence is a natural response to the needs of a society deeply preoccupied by "good living," by the surface appearance of existence. (On Sundays, off highways, in parking lots, in front of the clean angular houses, thousands of men, gripping Simoniz containers, polish their gleaming, swollen automobiles; their eyes glow; they seem as intent and devoted as lapidaries polishing old and precious stones.) But it scarcely follows that the presence of an entrenched craft tradition provides a salubrious climate for the artist. The artist is—or should be—concerned with a heightened sense of reality. He carries us beyond what we already know, intensifying and illuminating our deepest and most profound feelings. The craftsman, on the other hand, is interested in something else altogether: with the surface appearance of existence. He makes life more comfortable, pleasant, and engaging—or tries to. And his position in regard to art is revealed with sufficient clarity when he makes his appearance in the form of a modern architect who designs a house in which painting and sculpture have no place. (Some designers make room for a minuscule Klee on one wall; you have to look hard for it. It is usually a reproduction.)

So much, for the moment, for craft. Now until quite recently, American artists, whether they lived in California, New York, or states in between, felt a sharp necessity to pigeonhole themselves into one enclosure or another; I refer to the American School and the School of French Taste. Some successfully managed to wedge themselves into both compartments—Marin is an example; some with rather less effectiveness—Demuth is as good an example as any. But usually the haunting obsession with place, common to most artists, became overwhelming. Paris or the Great Plains? Cubism or the Ashcan School? This appalling and stifling either/or dilemma has been alarmingly demonstrated by the lives of a considerable number of somewhat feebly adjusted and centerless artists—the immediate contemporary parallel in another field is the radical turned Catholic (or vice versa)—

who "studied in Paris" and came home to reject with the greatest possible vehemence his culture-besmeared past and to paint, often enough with a similar vehemence, "the American scene."

More usually encountered was the avatar of French taste. Either by way of study abroad or through eager perusals of *Cahiers d'Art,* he soaked up the latest Parisian modes and submitted wholeheartedly to their example. He was often uneasy about the mere fact of being an American, thus continuing a long tradition of disquietude dating from colonial times, and he experienced a thrilling sense of awe in the presence of what he thought of as the towering aesthetic accomplishments current abroad. He was, in addition, an unswerving defender of the curious doctrine that the French are by nature more discerning of and hospitable to advanced trends than the inhabitants of any other spot on the globe.

If I seem to be ranging far afield from consideration of art in the bay region, I must protest that my course, however circuitously traced, is gauged to enclose precisely such considerations. But in order to talk about a species, one needs first to look a bit at the culture that produced the genus. As I have pointed out, one of the central concerns of most artists is the heightened consciousness of place. From the time of Copley through that of Hawthorne, Whistler, Mary Cassatt, Henry James, and on to the present, it has been a particular matter of import to American writers and painters. Where should one go? Where is the best place to work? In what kind of culture will the maximum nourishment be found?

San Francisco is not an art center in the usual sense of the term. Paris and New York are at present the only two such strongholds—swarming with artists, art galleries, and with a flourishing commercial activity based on the sale of painting and sculpture. Though twentieth-century art is largely the product of an urban or, more specifically, a metropolitan sensibility, it has been rather belatedly realized that residence in either Paris or New York is not a major requisite for producing works of art. Indeed, the last ten years have seen a radical change in the way in which many American artists regard such matters. I think it is particularly noticeable among some of the artists in San Francisco, where there are occasional glimmerings of a triumph over the obsession with place, or at least a rejection of the old choices. There is a recognition that the Spaniards Miró and Picasso, with their contempt for the myth of French taste, and the German Expressionists, who proceeded to ignore its existence, cut through to more open avenues than the one-way street of French taste. And there is an acceptance of the fact that the problems of art are more internal and central, and not to be solved by hints from Paris or from a residence abroad. Behind this attitude is no vestige of nationalism, parochialism, or regionalism. There is rather a willingness to accept help and influence from any source or place, whether it is South Africa, Munich, the South Seas, or across the street. The sentimentality of place has been abandoned; a phase has been lived through. And the person who today fancies Paris as a great aesthetic mother hen, hatching out all the art eggs, sums up a unique brand of parochialism: he has traded an area for the world.

Yet the culture—and I refer to the world at large—in a sociological or anthropological sense, remains very sick indeed. With our obsessive regard for specialization—a regard that is ridiculously the common ground of those in business, in the arts, and in the professions—the shared understanding of a larger universe is a concept that generates the coldest light conceivable. The used-car salesman sells his used car, the painter applies pigment to canvas, the osteopath manipulates a bone, the scientist builds a bomb or probes at a cancerous growth, the statesman signs a treaty. It is only reasonable that such a culture should produce so many who "don't know much about art, but know what they like," and who feel their skins crawl when exposed to any painting, poem, or musical composition that does not touch some nostalgic or commemorative source. And the relationship between the various branches of the arts, despite occasional well-meant attempts to bring them together, is in no less rickety shape. Surely one of the more disquieting aspects of our culture is the bland and unquestioning acceptance of the sickness. "I never read anything," says the painter. "I don't see what the painters today are up to," says the novelist. "Not that I don't admire modern painting. Vlaminck, Rouault. . . ."

Even so, a culture such as ours may—and does—produce works of art; it may be sick, but it is not sterile. And quite a few so-called "healthy" cultures have produced health but no works of art worth mentioning. R. G. Collingwood, the British philosopher, ordinarily so acute, has written* that the artist must "forego both entertainment value and magical value" to become the conscience of society. But isn't this precisely the trap into which Tolstoy stumbled in his old age? On the contrary, should not the artist employ every means in his power, including his own uniqueness, to be entertainer, magician, prophet, and conscience of society—as well as a good deal else? History sometimes settles for less; but the artist who consciously sets out to have experiences on behalf of large areas of the population, and to do only that, is not usually remembered for long. Collingwood has merely intellectualized the strategies of Kitsch.

What a specific locale will produce in the long run depends on the presence of men of great talent and ability, who are not too hampered or badgered to work productively and well. The San Francisco area has already produced, I believe, a few such men of promise, whose work extends a tradition and creates one of its own, rising above concerns with craft and above concerns that are either nationalistic, regional, or nourished alone by French taste. If we are beyond the point of hoping for a healthy culture, we can at least entertain a hope for a few small islands, crannies, nooks, here and there, where an art that is mature, serious, and unprovincial can come into being.

---

*The Principles of Art (Oxford: Oxford University Press, 1938).

American Taste and Whimsy

One of the remarkable aspects of taste is that no one, in my presence at least, has ever verbally admitted that his own taste is bad. Most of us have confessed at one time or another to past mistakes in judgment, timing, or decorum, to a lack of consideration, to bad manners, to moral laxity, and even—where taste is directly involved—to "lapses" of taste. These often have to do with miscalculations about the endurance value of a decorative or art object ("That Stamos I bought last year hasn't worn well at all. Bert thinks he can trade it to the Cutlers for that Congo mask they're so sick of." "After two years of Eames chairs, I couldn't be tireder; we're moving over to Robsjohn-Gibbings, and fast." "I don't know what I was thinking of when I picked out that wallpaper with the Scotties on it.") The point here is that corrections can always, or almost always, be made; but the basic individual taste remains eternally unquestioned. Even such bewildered parties as those who ultimately fall back on W. & J. Sloane to furnish their homes throughout and pay that firm to place its recognized aesthetic imprimatur on it, or those who ask the sofa salesman at Penney's to suggest an ottoman that "goes well," are only momentarily "uncertain"; they proclaim their faith in sources of true authority that can be turned to when an aesthetic choice becomes a problem.

And taste today, as Mr. Russell Lynes points out in his new book, is a large problem indeed:

Review of *The Tastemakers* by Russell Lynes, *New Republic,* January 17, 1955. Reprinted by permission.

The mere matter of how we decorate our homes is only a minor part of our concern. There are pressures on our tastes from all sides, pressures that even the most reluctant among us can scarcely ignore. The making of taste in America is, in fact, a major industry. Is there any other place that you can think of where there are so many professionals telling so many non-professionals what their taste should be? Is there any country which has as many magazines as we have devoted to telling people how they should decorate their homes, clothe their bodies, and deport themselves in company?

Probably not. The history of taste in this country is a large subject, and a fascinating one; Mr. Lynes's approach is by way of the persons and "forces" that have shaped American taste. It is a fair history, but not much more than that; it lacks both structure and a sense of continuity. Only events in this century and not all of the nineteenth are covered (Lynes begins in the last years of the 1820s when "the long period of control by . . . a landed and intellectual aristocracy" was ending) and his segmented treatment suggests a piecing together of magazine articles rather than an organic work. Some of his research is very impressive, and throughout the book, passages turn up that have material of considerable interest. *The Taste-makers* is the only work of its kind; but it is not in the same company with a similar book on the British, Sprague Allen's *Tides in English Taste,* a vastly more thorough, accurate, and entertaining piece of work. Mr. Francis Henry Taylor of the Metropolitan Museum has called *The Tastemakers* "a mature and thoughtful book . . . often very profound." *De gustibus,* of course but look at the taste of Mr. Francis Henry Taylor, not only by way of his writings on art but as set forth in the redecorating job at the Metropolitan, with its Dorothy Draper modrun dining room, white and chartreuse, with cold chicken patties and a pervasive sense of even deeper chills surrounding them.

It would nevertheless be a mistake not to appreciate the skill and time that Mr. Lynes has expended on such figures as the landscape architect Andrew Jackson Downing, such early collectors as Luman Reed and Thomas Jefferson Bryan, or Charles Lock Eastlake, the author of *Hints on Household Taste*

(1872), and Elise de Wolfe, who spread her decorative ideas across the country, from the Crockers of San Francisco to the Weyerhausers of Minneapolis and on to the Fifth Avenue mansion of Henry C. Frick. Even so skimpy an account of the Armory Show as the one Mr. Lynes has set down has a certain value, and his chapter on the suburbs is one of the best things in his book.

But it struck me that what Mr. Lynes has borne down on most heavily is not taste, but whim. Lynes is not so much interested in "tastemakers" as he is in the amusement to be provided through the changing styles and fads promoted by commercial interests in the fields of painting, design, architecture, and interior decoration. It could probably not have been otherwise, since Mr. Lynes says that he does not know what taste is, that no one is capable of defining taste, and that he is quite in the dark about what *good* taste is. With this kind of an approach—and with ourselves equally blank as to what Mr. Lynes's own tastes are—it is hard to know what he is getting at when he writes that "taste in itself is nothing. It is only what taste leads to that makes any difference in our lives." But where? Mr. Lynes apparently has some kind of desire to indicate a sense of direction, but his index finger waves and wanders. About all that he can conclude is that people worry about taste too much and should stop it.

But I am not sure that I understand Mr. Lynes. One of his specialities has been the rough categorizing of human beings into the divisions of lowbrow, middlebrow, and highbrow. His famous piece of some years ago is reprinted here, in which he is by turns patronizing, Olympian, condescending, and severe about "highbrows," annoyed or amused by "middlebrows" (but not if they happen to be *his* kind of middlebrow), and more of the same about lowbrows. In what pigeonhole does Mr. Lynes place himself? We never know. Reading *The Taste-makers* is rather like talking to someone who tells endless stories about other people—some of them amusing, some ironic, and some merely informative, but who is careful never to commit himself. It is hard to deal with the issues raised by questions of taste if you are, like Mr. Lynes, so organized that you appear, on one hand, to dislike the democratization of taste, and, on the other, are contemptuous of the "highbrows"—even a highbrow that Mr. Lynes creates in much the way that Frankenstein created a monster.

What Mr. Lynes appears to dislike most about "highbrows" is that some of them are impatient with frivolity in the arts. But Mr. Lynes himself is pretty impatient, almost irritable, with someone like Mr. Clement Greenberg, who performed as a "tastemaker" in a very real and active sense for many years, repeatedly sticking out his neck for artists he admired when the magazines, museums, and the general public were indifferent or contemptuous toward them. And Lynes rarely steers in the direction of many actual "tastemakers" of this or any other kind—toward men such as Walter Arensberg and John Quinn, art collectors and patrons of the arts of an independent cast of mind that have almost vanished; toward men who not only had taste but knew how to express it and had something to say about it—Tocqueville, Henry James, Randolph Bourne, Paul Rosenfeld, and Gilbert Seldes, for instance.

We have to assume, in these matters, that some people know more than others—just as we know that Stravinsky knows more about music than the leader of a Boy Scout band in Kansas—that the taste of a Matisse was superior to that of a Rockwell Kent, that Erich von Stroheim's taste ranges wider than Stanley Kramer's or Joe Pasternak's, and that Ezra Pound's goes beyond any of the Benêts. Mr. Lynes says that the "highbrow"—a figure who gets dimmer to me before he gets clearer—is "devoted to the proposition that the arts must be pigeonholed." Who? Mr. Lynes pigeonholes human beings.

The Interesting Lives They Lead

I suppose that everyone thinks that his life is interesting to some extent or the suicide rate would be even higher than it is; consider the number of persons who keep journals, diaries, write their autobiographies or talk about the most humdrum aspects of their days to each other or even pay for the privilege of doing so in the company of such professional listeners as psychiatrists. I am willing to be persuaded that every life *is* interesting, but not in terms of the manner in which most current autobiographies are being written. Nor am I thinking of, exactly, Henry Adams, Casanova, Barbellion, or even Rousseau.

Mr. Vernon Duke is a very accomplished writer of popular tunes ("I Can't Get Started with You," "What Is There to Say?" and "April in Paris" are among the best-known tunes) and a talented composer along what are considered more serious lines. He is original; and, as he says, his versatility

> . . . has in reality been infuriating to most musical people. Just why that is I have no way of knowing, but the critical boys seem to think there is something monstrous and unnatural about a composer writing two different kinds of music under two different names. [Duke was christened Vladimir Dukelsky.] It annoys them not to be able to say that I go slumming when writing jazz, and it annoys them still more not to be able to classify me as an ambitious peasant, gazing at the musical Olympus behind a Lindy's herring.

Review of *Passport to Paris* by Vernon Duke, *New Republic*, June 20, 1955. Reprinted by permission.

He has more than one side, which an age of specialization finds puzzling or irritating and sometimes suspicious. He has been closely associated with Prokofiev, Stravinsky, Auric, Diaghilev, and George Gershwin, and the list of people he has known in the theater, musical comedy, ballet, and Tin Pan Alley runs, in the index, from Alex Aarons to Vera Zorina. Duke *has* had an "interesting life," much of which I would like to know a great deal more about. But like the majority of the autobiographies of contemporaries that are appearing at present—whether they issue from the typewriters of society figures, ministers, industrial wizards, newspaper publishers, or the operators of call-houses, Duke's account takes its stylistic cues not too remotely from the gossip columnists and the magazines designed to be read on streetcars and subways. And a good deal of the time there is this kind of glistening recollection:

> I was the first to enter the de Meyer drawing room—a regrettable mistake, as no one *divin* is ever punctual. My embarrassment was somewhat relieved by the cordiality of my hosts and the perfection of the dry Martini I was offered, a drink still misunderstood by Parisians, who call it *un dry*—pronounced "dree"—and make it almost entirely of vermouth, using gin as sparingly as if it were Fernet Branca. Some small talk followed, very small indeed on my part, and then Sergei Pavlovitch entered with Boris in tow, both splendidly shaven and eau-de-cologned.
>
> That night I dried my first, and probably last, tears of happiness and realized that Victorian novelists had something there, for never did tears taste so sweet to me. What ensued was equally dreamlike. . . .

There is quite a lot of this, and it has the charm of Elinor Glyn at times, of *The Young Visitors,* of the imitators of Firbank and all the confessions of the many young men who wrote about Paris in the twenties.

Names are dropped with such ease and rapidity as to suggest a string of beads breaking, and Duke makes no apologies for this; I suppose it is the figure in his particular carpet. It is only with effort, though, that one can associate the owners of the names with the persons they designate. And I suppose it is without point to hope for, in this kind of account, any sense of formal structure and harmonics that one automatically anticipates—or used to anticipate—in a poem or in a piece of music, or very much less, in the novel (where one's expectations these days are more spectacularly withered). This is a time when "raw experience" is infinitely more palatable than the orchestration of experience. One of the few recent autobiographies that attempted to make a work of art out of a life—Conrad Aiken's *Ushant*—quickly found its way into the stockrooms of the remainder houses.

There are not many books that deal with popular music, and Duke's is most valuable for what he has to say about writing music for the theater, the commercial aspects of show business and song-publishing, and the occasional bright portraits of men he has known—particularly Stravinsky and Diaghilev and Gershwin. Before writing *Passport to Paris*, Duke tells us that he read

> . . . a great many autobiographies, particularly those of my contemporaries. I have discovered that autobiographies can roughly be divided into two groups, those with emphasis on facts and those preoccupied with literary style. Sir Osbert Sitwell is a good sample of the second type, and Tallulah Bankhead and Agnes de Mille are typical of the first school. . . . As for me, I thought a great deal about a tongue-in-cheek approach, the poker-face approach, the Dali or sensational-at-all-costs approach, the Freud or turn-over-a-new-fig-leaf approach, and finally decided to stick to the facts and the hell with it.

More or less routine is the word. Duke's music has always been tasteful and smart; too little even of that spills over into his prose.

Muskrat Ramble
Popular and Unpopular Music

. . .in the ripe olives the very circumstances of their being near rottenness adds a peculiar beauty to the fruit.

It is midafternoon. I come away from the window and the rooftops and turn the knob on the radio that sends a thin line cutting across the rows of numbers. I would like to hear, say, Jelly Roll Morton playing "The Crave," but will settle for a Lee Wiley record; except for a station on which a voice not easily distinguishable from Miss Margaret Truman's is singing "At Dawning" and another on which a program of "light classics" by a feeble string group emerges oppressively distinct, all the other stations are playing record after record by big dance bands. Claude Thornhill, Kay Kyser, Tex Beneke, Charlie Spivak, Vaughn Monroe. I switch off the radio and go into the other room to pour myself a drink.

We live in a time of triumphant demonstrations of the three laws Mr. Nock found so illuminating: Epstean's law (people satisfy their needs and desires with the least possible exertion), Gresham's (bad money drives out good money), and the law of diminishing returns.

For the last ten years or more, a period that has been sufficiently dispiriting for both High and Popular Culture, it has still been possible, though the occasions of possibility have been rare enough, for some works of value to emerge. In High Culture, individual writers, painters, and composers,

---

From *The Scene Before You, 1955,* edited by Chandler Brossard (New York: Rinehart, 1955). This is the revised version of an essay originally published in *Partisan Review* 15 (May, 1948). Reprinted by permission.

most of them isolated as so many bears in winter, have gone on working, and in climates colder than most bears care for. Although Gresham's law in particular has continued to function with the efficiency and drive of a supercharged bone-crusher, it has had to cope with one factor that alone has kept the world from becoming a cultural Nagasaki—the granitelike recalcitrance of these figures of High Culture. It is all that stands between what little we have left and a world completely at the mercy of the John Steinbecks, Eli Siegmeisters, Fibber McGees, Leon Krolls, and Henry Seidel Canbys.

High Culture, although it has been subject to the same accelerated tendencies toward decay that kept Henry Adams awake and put the world to sleep, still has a kind of life, however spasmodic its successes and however hemmed in by the all but completely victorious Middle Culture that takes what it can assimilate both from High and Popular Culture for the purpose of mashing them to death.

But Popular Culture is completely at the mercy of the laws hastening corruption and decay. Popular Culture must *go along*. No other road is open. Unlike High Art, it cannot fall back on attitudes of recalcitrance for survival. Lloyd, Hamilton, W. C. Fields, Buster Keaton—comedians of wit, humanity, and situation, for instance, give way to verbalizing gagsters: Bob Hope, Milton Berle, Red Skelton.* The comic strip evolves into a series of continued stories that are linear replicas of soap operas and the pulps; and similar patterns tiredly repeat themselves in every field of Popular Culture.

If the laws of which I have spoken could themselves speak, however, their proudest boast would be reserved for the debasement of popular music. Here is total capitulation. The period from the end of the First World War to about 1936 was one of enormous productivity of first-rate tunes; month

---

*Fields, toward the end of his life (like Chaplin today) became increasingly savage in his satire, and an audience that wanted nothing but reassurance could only respond uneasily, baffled and repelled; eventually it turned away from him. Along these lines, the reception of Chaplin's last film has been very instructive.

after month accounted for numbers that are still fresh after a decade of repetition. Even David Rose has done his worst and left them relatively untouched. The period represents a flowering that has few comparable examples in the Popular Arts. But after 1936 the drought set in. The last ten years, so far as popular music is concerned, have been bleak. From around 1920 to 1936: "Exactly Like You," "Thou Swell," "Tea for Two," "My Fate Is in Your Hands," "Honeysuckle Rose," "April in Paris," "Avalon," "Get Out of Town," "I Never Knew," "Nice Work If You Can Get It," "Baby Won't You Please Come Home," "Fascinatin' Rhythm," "The Man I Love," "Just One of Those Things," "Yesterdays," "On the Sunny Side of the Street," "Cherry," "It Had to Be You," "There'll Be Some Changes Made," "You Do Something to Me," "Moanin' Low," "I Know That You Know," "Liza," "My One and Only," "Embraceable You," "Someone to Watch Over Me," "Memories of You," "Lady Be Good," "I Can't Get Started with You" (written by Vernon Duke and Ira Gershwin in 1936—about the last gasp of the period), "My Kinda Love," "Time on My Hands," "Concentratin' on You," "Delilah," "Rose Room," "Body and Soul," "After You've Gone," "Old Fashioned Love," "Keepin' Myself for You"—a much-truncated list, but one that includes most of the tunes on which some jazz performers and everyone on down from there—including the large, ponderously stringed music-to-read-by *schmalz* combinations—have depended most heavily.

A handful of men wrote most of them: Gershwin, Spencer, Williams, Fats Waller, Youmans, Cole Porter, Rodgers and Hart. Most of these men are dead; there have been no successors. (Out of an earlier jazz period that stretched into the twenties came such impressive and enduring hot classics as "Wolverine Blues," "King Porter Stomp," "Ballin' the Jack," "Shake That Thing," "Dippermouth," "Shreveport Stomp," "Snag It," "Mamie's Blues," "Mabel's Dream," "Gimme a Pigfoot," "Original Rags," "Euphonic Sounds," "Steamboat Stomp," "The Pearls," "Snake Rag," among a great many more. Almost everything written by Jelly Roll Morton, King Oliver, Scott Joplin, Clarence Williams, Jimmy Blythe—most of them musicians and band leaders of a very high order—

remains fresh and robust. Men of their quality belong to a time as enclosed and without continuance as that of the Ephrata Cloisters, Vorticism, or the demesne of Lord Timothy Dexter.) Today from the broken tap that Cole Porter turns on at widely spaced intervals leak repetitive imitations of his earlier smooth flow. Vernon Duke's more recent work—show tunes, largely —is not the sort of thing that interests recording directors, unfortunately. Duke Ellington interests himself in musical embroidery work. He has also recently become a disc jockey and plays some of the most richly debased stuff ever committed to wax. Richard Rodgers composes music for operettas like *Oklahoma* and *Allegro,* a very sad end. Harold Arlen, responsible for such unfaded period pieces as "Fun to Be Fooled," "You Said It," "Moanin' in the Morning," and "Down with Love," has eliminated from his work his early originality and spontaneity.

The general drift of songwriters to the West Coast since the introduction of sound films has had its effects. In Hollywood, Epstean's law finds its purest expression. Songwriters, malleable as margarine, easily made happy by residences convenient to a racetrack, have lived up to the pattern. Hollywood Hit Parade—juke box—Hooperized numbers, tailored to blanket the country and ravel out in four weeks, become all-pervading models. Just as large sections of industry seem to be consciously aiming at the creation of overpriced jimcrack merchandise—expensive fountain pens that feed great blots on one's stationery, alarm clocks that fail to go off, shirts that turn to ribbons after three washings, toothpaste that brings on gingivitis, chinaware that disintegrates in the dishwater, so does the songwriting industry aggrandize the ephemeral as it ransacks the most barren and unserviceable ideas of the past. "Imitation diamonds," wrote Tocqueville over one hundred years ago, "are now made which easily may be mistaken for real ones; as soon as the art of fabricating false diamonds shall have reached so high a degree of perfection that they cannot be distinguished from real ones, it is probable that both one and the other will be abandoned, and become mere pebbles again." Tocqueville's prediction has yet to be realized; the relevance of his metaphor persists. Songwriters of late have attempted only the imitation of imitations.

The nervous, gay, compulsive music of the twenties gives way to a tastelessness streamlined beyond belief. Gershwin and some of his contemporaries were greatly gifted men *for what they were doing,* expressing simple emotions with a freshness of melodic and harmonic ideas and with a particular sense of joy that the thirties buried (enthralled Stalinist gravediggers wielding albums of Josh White and the Red Army Chorus under their arms; "folk" operettists; novelty swing combinations; exponents of calculated corn; floy-floy hysterics; the composers of the song "everyone" is whistling— "Chi Baba Chi Baba," "Chickory Chick," "Open the Door Richard," "Pistol Packin' Mama," "People Will Say We're in Love," "Jingle Jangle Jingle," "Deep in the Heart of Texas," "There'll Be Bluebirds over the White Cliffs of Dover," "I'll Dance at Your Wedding"—an endless and unspeakable catalogue). There are few more dependable methods of obtaining a quick migraine than by merely reading over a list of the hit tunes of the last ten or twelve years.

Monolithic symbol of the whole period is the juke box: this permanent guest in public places that squats like some ominous and temporarily static beast, afoam with lights and tubes of colored water; it might have been built by André Breton in collaboration with some monstrously sick and divided opponent of industrialism who had spent a claustrophobic lifetime in Greek candy stores. There it sits, booming or silently awaiting a nickel, ready with "A Rainy Night in Rio" and Perry Como, where the piano player used to be, his cigarette turning the ivories of the upper register a sickly Mars yellow. He was not often a good pianist, but he knew more tunes than the twenty the juke box knows; and you could talk to him.

Compared with the music currently being written, musical performance is deceptively healthy. Even the best jazz today lacks the fresh originating intelligence at work in the late twenties; and the best musicians are now only extending and developing patterns of improvisation laid out during the early quarter of this century. There is an immense concern with mere preservation. The unearthing, several years ago, of Bunk Johnson, probably the oldest living pioneer of jazz, who had dropped out of music and had to be provided with a set of new teeth before his triumphant comeback, was a welcome act of antiquarian recovery. Johnson's long-buried and pure turn-of-the-century New Orleans style served as a landmark from which to view almost fifty years of jazz mutations and variants. Johnson's more impassioned admirers correctly placed great emphasis on his astonishing power and wide-open tone, alive with personal feeling. These almost compensated for an inventive deficiency that made for considerable monotony as chorus followed chorus.

It has been the practice of some later musicians to work intensively at the inventive, though feeling has often been buried in displays of virtuosity. Performers such as Tony Parenti, Don Ewell, Paul Lingle, Bob Helm, Wally Rose, Burt Bales, Turk Murphy, among others,* continue to resist corruption; but their ranks are systematically being thinned out by desertions for cushier swing bands, by sudden collapses of talent, and the normal high death rate among jazz musicians, whose occupational hazards include heart attacks, malnutrition, and a recurrent pattern of drunkenness and sudden death of pneumonia in Middle Western cities.

More than a few go on playing well; the difficulties of hearing them continue to multiply. Manhattan's Fifty-second Street, once as devoted to night clubs featuring jazz and jam sessions as Grand Street is to wedding gowns or Bleecker

---

*The *Partisan Review* text lists: "Armstrong, James P. Johnson, Kid Ory, Barney Bigard, Art Tatum, Earl Hines, Bechet, Jack Teagarden, Georg Brunis, Ben Webster, and a good many of the Chicago stylists clustered around Eddie Condon." In the revised list of 1955 Kees reveals a more personal selection influenced by the traditional jazz revival that occurred in San Francisco at this time. Some of these men were acquainted with Kees, an accomplished pianist himself. He occasionally jammed with Turk Murphy, a San Francisco bandleader and the most important figure in the revival. With Bob Helm, another local musician, Kees collaborated on a number of compositions as a lyricist.—ED.

Street to salami, makes way for replacements in the form of office buildings, expensive clubs, business establishments, and tourist night spots with "intimate" singers and Hawaiian dancing girls. Four years ago there was at least one night club in New York that offered first-rate jazz, unwatered and non-poisonous liquor at reasonable prices, and a quiet crowd that did not come there to have their photographs taken, their caricatures drawn, or to annoy the musicians. This was the Pied Piper, on Barrow Street, in the Village. For a brief period, when it first opened, it offered a memorable five-piece group that included Max Kaminsky, the late Rod Cless on clarinet, Frank Orchard on valve trombone, and, as inter-mission pianist and at the top of his form, the remarkable, vastly influential, and still underrated James J. Johnson. There is nothing remotely like the Pied Piper left in New York. Indifferent music, high prices, poor liquor, or com-binations of this trinity have taken over everywhere. The rash of jazz "concerts" in such places as Town Hall have not been very satisfactory substitutes. The musicians, along with the more ravaged-looking members of the audience, wear ex-pressions of strain brought on by the absence of a bar and by a milieu too little enclosed. At various times, attempts have been made to present regular programs of good jazz on the air—notably those conducted by Condon and by Rudi Blesh; but from the start their chances of commercial sponsorship were as remote as those of Wallace Stevens's appearing as a regular contributor in *Collier's*. The networks made short work of both programs.

While jazz persists on records and occasionally elsewhere, the best of it increasingly nostalgic, depending more and more on a cultist rather than on a popular base, it is almost drowned out by the racket of the large swing and popular bands. These have next to nothing to do with jazz, although they often contain remnants of rather gratuitous jazz in solo work (the best of these bands, Artie Shaw's and Benny Good-man's, are gone). Standard practice today in the search for trade-marks and novelty is the isolation of some rhythmic pattern, tonal element, or harmonic trickery to vulgarize and thus "build up" a "style." Hence "rippling rhythms," slinky piano effects, fixated use of a series of augmented chords, musical statements that are so surfacy that they beg the question of feeling at all. The Stan Kenton band is a good example of tremendous effort going into the creation of such a style, through echo chamber effects and hollow intimations of Debussy and Stravinsky.

Enormously popular just now are the relaxed Cream of Wheat–Gerber Baby Food instrumental trios, usually piano, guitar, and string bass, with one man singing empty little jump tunes. There are dozens of these, all playing at a volume undeviating as a cat's purr. This music had its origin, I would guess, in the dimly lit night clubs of the East Fifties, where it served, and still serves, the purpose of covering up dead spots in the conversation. Like the music that dominated the period in the late 1700s just before the revolutionary music of Gluck, it was not originally intended to be listened to at all. Millions now follow it, over the air and on records.

And now, finally, we come to those who play in the latest and extravagantly acclaimed manner variously labeled Be-Bob, bebop, and rebop. Here is a full-fledged cult. Its more orthodox devotees even model their appearance on that of Dizzy Gillespie, bebop's pioneer and bellwether, a goateed trumpet player who wears a beret, horn-rimmed glasses, and neckties with his own not very appealing countenance painted thereon. Iconoclastic and compulsive types, many bebop cultists extend their interests beyond music—to drug-addiction, abstract painting, and the theories (and for all I know the practice) of Wilhelm Reich, philosopher of the orgasm. Some beboppers are interested in the close textual critics of poetry; I learned from a friend whom I believe to be reliable that one such fan announced that Cleanth Brooks is "definitely hip"— a term of warm approval.

The beboppers or hipsters are, however, a great deal more interesting than bebop itself. Yet they offer the most insistent testimonies to bebop's superiority to other kinds of music. " 'Do you dig Dizzy?' is fast becoming the musician's counterpart to 'Do you speak English?' " writes Mr. Mort Schillinger in *Downbeat*, in the characteristic razzmatazz style of the swing magazines. "Never before in the history of Jazz has so dynamic a person as Dizzy Gillespie gained the spotlight of acclaim and idolization . . . from the humblest of the unknown to the heights of huzza at which he stands today. With the waxing of Hawk's [Coleman Hawkins's] *Body and Soul* . . . Jazz reached a pinnacle of development. The human imagination has its limitations, just as the human arm or leg, and Jazz had reached the point where the musician's imagination could no longer function effectively without the added stimulus of new horizons for exploitation. There were two alternatives: either Jazz could remain stagnant and in time lose its identity as a highly creative art, or it could develop new facets for the imagination, new stimuli to artistic fabrication. Fortunately it followed the latter course—chose it and assigned the task to Dizzy Gillespie." Mr. Schillinger goes on to remark Gillespie's "genius for substituting and extending chords in unorthodox but singularly thrilling ways and places [and] Dizzy's entirely original articulation and phrasing, which is hardly describable through the medium of the printed word without recourse to highly technical terminology. . . ."

Mr. Rudi Blesh, in a recent piece in the *Herald Tribune,* is more controlled. "Seeming non-sequiturs can be artfully combined to express an integrated idea, and this method, a psychological one, is common in modern music and literature. But the irrelevant parts of bebop are exactly what they seem; they add up to no such unity. . . . A capricious and neurotically rhapsodic sequence of effects for their own sake, [bebop] comes perilously close to complete nonsense as a musical expression. . . . Far from a culmination of jazz, bebop is not jazz at all but an ultimately degenerated form of swing, exploiting the most fantastic rhythms and unrelated harmonies that it would seem possible to conceive."

I have been listening to bebop on occasion for several years now, and lately, as I started work on this piece, listening with more strict attention; and I can only report, very possibly because of some deeply buried strain of black reaction in me, that I have found this music uniformly thin, at once dilapidated and overblown, and exhibiting a poverty of thematic development and a richness of affectation not only, apparently, intentional, but enormously self-satisfied. Whole-tone progressions and triple-tongued runs are worked relentlessly, far beyond the saturation point. There has been nothing like this in the way of an overconsciousness of stylistic idiosyncrasy, I should say, since the Gothic Revival. Although bebop's defenders reserve as their trump card this music's "element of the unexpected," it is precisely bebop's undeviating pattern of incoherence and limitation that makes it predictable in the extreme, and ultimately as boring as the projects of Gutzon Borglum.

In Paris, where Erskine Caldwell, Steinbeck, Henry Miller, and Horace McCoy are best sellers and "nobody reads Proust anymore," where the post-Picasso painters have sunk into torpor and repetition, and where intellectuals are more cynically Stalinized than in any other city in the world, bebop is vastly admired. Evidently Gresham's and Epstean's laws work with equal severity in other countries besides the United States, although a lot of people are taking Christ's own time finding it out.*

---

*This was written in 1948. Since that time, my ideas on the subject have changed a good deal, and so has the music. Recording directors and engineers with stopwatches, publishers unable to read music who listen only to "demonstration" records of tunes (preferably high fidelity), A&R men who stress technical quality at the expense of music, are firmly in control at the large recording companies. Many small labels have made an appearance, and some of them—Riverside, Fantasy, Good Time Jazz, and "X," among others—have been markedly successful in marketing both reissues and some new material. A fresh interest in New Orleans revivalism is growing. Bebop has given way to "progressive" and "cool" music. And the hit parade kind of tune has become even more vacuous than it was in 1948, stressing repetition, witless lyrics, and self-pity.

How to Be Happy
Installment 1053

Something is always new and remarkable to someone. I remember an acquaintance hurrying up to me one day some years ago and exclaiming, "I've just found the most remarkable novelist! What a discovery! You've got to read him!" He caught me in a receptive mood and I asked who this person might be. "He's a writer named Dostoevsky," he confided.

Dr. Arnold A. Hutschnecker is a little like that. In our present atmosphere of distrust, violence, and irrationality, with so many human beings murdering themselves—either literally or symbolically—Dr. Hutschnecker, an M.D. of New York and Sherman, Connecticut, has written a book that offers itself as one that will "help you to find a happier life by recognizing and resolving . . . your basic loves and hates." His answer, which he sounds as if he had just discovered, is psychology!

> Each age has its bright new precept for changing the world. . . .
> Are we arrogant in believing that it will achieve what other concepts have failed to do? Actually we are confident because it gives us for the first time an understanding of the deeper levels of human nature. This new knowledge is revolutionary. It offers a hope that is not static but dynamic. It is not the kind of hope indulged in by those who want much and do little, but it is a creative hope that attains its goal by understanding and hard

Review of *Love and Hate in Human Nature* by Arnold A. Hutschnecker, M.D., *New Republic,* July 18, 1955. Reprinted by permission.

work. Furthermore, psychology shows us how we can not only *understand* but change our behavior.

This bright new precept, however, has a rather worn and haggard air by now. Psychology in a historical sense is scarcely a novelty, although Dr. Hutschnecker seems to share the conviction of many that some particular value is attached to an idea by way of its having been recently developed—or come upon. Systematic psychology is a late nineteenth-century development; and the sort of book that the Doctor has written is very much in the tradition of hundreds of such books that appeared in the 1920s, designed to move Freud painlessly into the American living room. André Tridon, "the physician of the soul," Harvey O'Higgins, and James Oppenheim were only a few who came proffering their keys to emotional salvation through "self-knowledge."

The Doctor is undismayed by this time-lapse and sings his old music with a brave nostalgic air. A chorus of praising voices—with a certain amount of orchestration, one can imagine, from the Doctor's publisher—are currently chiming in the background. They include physicians (one of them, a Fordham man, says that it "reads like a novel"), a psychiatrist, the novelist Laura Z. Hobson ("insight," says Mrs. Hobson), and such witnesses as screen actresses Ella Raines and Janis Paige.

Here, then, is another how-to-do-it book, another guide to peace of mind and "self-understanding." A rough approximation of Freud is set forth, even more pat, perhaps, than usual, with promises of results that are dependable and certain. Freudianism and "science" are equated. "As science banishes the ignorance that was the cause of many of our difficulties," Dr. Hutschnecker writes, "we see the beginning of a miracle. Man who has been an automaton for so long, is at last gaining an awareness of himself and of his role as a human being." It is interesting to see how science and the miraculous are brought together here, and even more so to consider a little such automata as Renaissance men, for instance, with their distressing lack of self-awareness and ignorance of roles.

The critical and highly self-questioning attitudes of many contemporary psychiatrists, who have not found the techniques of Freud of much help in understanding or treating schizophrenics, are not for Dr. Hutschnecker. A heavy-handed emphasis on Bleuler's concept of ambivalence—the "conflict" of love and hate—serves instead; and there are a number of case histories, in which the Doctor's patients do not turn out at all badly.

There is also a surprising amount of actual misinformation, such as the Doctor's statement that we "are the only animals who attack our own kind." One thinks of wolves, monkeys, many of the birds of prey, a large variety of insects, male bears that try to kill their young, to mention only a few examples. The Doctor's view of the relationship of the sexes may be viewed by some as rather assertively military, for he writes that the "struggle between the male and female is the most relentless war of which we have any knowledge. None of the wars in history can match it in obstinacy, neither the savage religious campaigns of the middle ages nor ferocious civil wars."

If Dr. Hutschnecker is not to be depended on for his knowledge of animal behavior, and if his comparisions verge on the extreme, his insight into particular examples of human behavior also leaves a good deal to be desired. Is the kind of "insight" Dr. Hutschnecker has to offer such an improvement on the insights of Pascal, Baudelaire, or Ecclesiastes? It would seem open to question, at least, whether the clinical conception of the Oedipus Complex and sex-jealousy, castration-anxiety and all the rest are the chief determinants of character and culture, or that they give us "understanding" "for the first time" or even that they represent beacon lights on the way to Dr. Hutschnecker's "age old dream of peace."

Dr. Hutschnecker is all on the side, however, of "self-knowledge." Now no one, so far as I know, is against self-knowledge, within limits; and few are dubious about it—except, perhaps, dramatists of the order of Sophocles and Shakespeare, or any poet with a tragic sense, or a great many philosophers, or such a writer as Ford Madox Ford, who wrote one of the great novels on the subject of love and hate, or perhaps the man who said that a little learning is a dangerous thing.

The Doctor offers self-knowledge as a set of rules, gimmicks essentially, and concludes with a list of numbered "basic beliefs" to get us through these times of strain. "Respect for Life," "Reason for Life," "Responsibility," "Tolerance," "Adjustment" are some of them—and there are probably not many who will deny that these are all qualities worth attaining. Presented as they are here, however, "self-knowledge" is turned into a mere by-product of "modern psychology," with the Doctor's assumption that "we are now able to penetrate the mystery of the unconscious self."

Have we? Has Doctor Hutschnecker? Socrates, Proust, and Coleridge, for instance, had more "self-knowledge" and knew more at first hand of love and hate than the Doctor will ever know; they also wrote very well indeed, unlike the Doctor, and with greater reverence and humility; and they never believed for a moment that "self-knowledge" could, in the long run, save them—or us. With all his wisdom, Socrates had one of the most horrendous domestic lives on record and was sentenced to death for his ideas; Proust's masterpiece came out of an existence of incredible emotional suffering; Coleridge found release in opium. The liberal assumption that self-knowledge will lead to "adjustment" and "happiness" is a curious one; it is not very inspiriting to see it presented in terms of "science," as Doctor Hutschnecker does. I have frequently wondered what course psychiatry would have taken if it had developed out of the humanities rather than medicine. Dr. Hutschnecker's book had me speculating even more.